TABLE OF CONTENTS

Top 20 Test Taking Tips

1. Carefully follow all the test registration procedures
2. Know the test directions, duration, topics, question types, how many questions
3. Setup a flexible study schedule at least 3-4 weeks before test day
4. Study during the time of day you are most alert, relaxed, and stress free
5. Maximize your learning style; visual learner use visual study aids, auditory learner use auditory study aids
6. Focus on your weakest knowledge base
7. Find a study partner to review with and help clarify questions
8. Practice, practice, practice
9. Get a good night's sleep; don't try to cram the night before the test
10. Eat a well balanced meal
11. Know the exact physical location of the testing site; drive the route to the site prior to test day
12. Bring a set of ear plugs; the testing center could be noisy
13. Wear comfortable, loose fitting, layered clothing to the testing center; prepare for it to be either cold or hot during the test
14. Bring at least 2 current forms of ID to the testing center
15. Arrive to the test early; be prepared to wait and be patient
16. Eliminate the obviously wrong answer choices, then guess the first remaining choice
17. Pace yourself; don't rush, but keep working and move on if you get stuck
18. Maintain a positive attitude even if the test is going poorly
19. Keep your first answer unless you are positive it is wrong
20. Check your work, don't make a careless mistake

Mathematics Section

A detailed knowledge of algebra and trigonometry is NOT necessary to answer to succeed on TABE Mathematics section. Don't be intimidated by the questions presented. They do not require highly advanced math knowledge, but only the ability to recognize basic problems types and apply simple formulas and methods to solving them.

That is our goal, to show you the simple formulas and methods to solving these problems, so that while you will not gain a mastery of math from this guide, you will learn the methods necessary to succeed on the TABE. This guide attacks problems that are simple in nature but may have been glossed over during your education.

- All numbers used are real numbers.
- Figures or drawings beside questions are provided as additional information that should be useful in solving the problem. They are drawn fairly accurately, unless the figure is noted as "not drawn to scale".
- Jagged or straight lines can both be assumed to be straight.
- Unless otherwise stated, all drawings and figures lie in a plane.

Solving for Variables

Variables are letters that represent an unknown number. You must solve for that unknown number in single variable problems. The main thing to remember is that you can do anything to one side of an equation as long as you do it to the other.

Example: Solve for x in the equation $2x + 3 = 5$.
Answer: First you want to get the "2x" isolated by itself on one side. To do that, first get rid of the 3. Subtract 3 from both sides of the equation $2x + 3 - 3 = 5 - 3$ or $2x = 2$. Now since the x is being multiplied by the 2 in "2x", you must divide by 2 to get rid of it. So, divide both sides by 2, which gives $2x / 2 = 2 / 2$ or $x = 1$.

- 6 -

Drawings

Other problems may describe a geometric shape, such as a triangle or circle, but may not include a drawing of the shape. TABE is testing whether you can read a description and make appropriate inferences by visualizing the object and related information. There is a simple way to overcome this obstacle. DRAW THE SHAPE! A good drawing (or even a bad drawing) is much easier to understand and interpret than a brief description.

Make a quick drawing or sketch of the shape described. Include any angles or lengths provided in the description. Once you can see the shape, you have already partially solved the problem and will be able to determine the right answer.

Positive/Negative Numbers

Multiplication/Division

A negative multiplied or divided by a negative = a positive number.

Example: -3 * -4 = 12; -6 / -3 = 2

A negative multiplied by a positive = a negative number.

Example: -3 * 4 = -12; -6 / 3 = -2

Addition/Subtraction

Treat a negative sign just like a subtraction sign.

Example: 3 + -2 = 3 – 2 or 1

Remember that you can reverse the numbers while adding or subtracting.

Example: -4+2 = 2 + -4 = 2 – 4 = -2

A negative number subtracted from another number is the same as adding a positive number.

Example: 2 - -1 = 2 + 1 = 3

Beware of making a simple mistake!

Example: An outdoor thermometer drops from 42º to – 8º. By how many degrees has the outside air cooled?

Answer: A common mistake is to say 42º – 8º = 34º, but that is wrong. It is actually 42º - - 8º or 42º + 8º = 50º

Exponents

When exponents are multiplied together, the exponents are added to get the final result.

Example: $x*x = x^2$, where x^1 is implied and $1 + 1 = 2$.

When exponents in parentheses have an exponent, the exponents are multiplied to get the final result.

Example: $(x^3)^2 = x^6$, because $3*2 = 6$.

Another way to think of this is that $(x^3)^2$ is the same as $(x^3)*(x^3)$. Now you can use the multiplication rule given above and add the exponents, $3 + 3 = 6$, so $(x^3)^2 = x^6$

Decimal Exponents (aka Scientific Notation)

This usually involves converting back and forth between scientific notation and decimal numbers (e.g. 0.02 is the same as 2×10^{-2}). There's an old "cheat" to this problem: if the number is less than 1, the number of digits behind the decimal point is the same as the exponent that 10 is raised to in scientific notation, except that the exponent is a negative number; if the number is greater than 1, the exponent of 10 is equal to the number of digits ahead of the decimal point minus 1.

Example: Convert 3000 to decimal notation.

Answer: 3×10^3, since 4 digits are ahead of the decimal, the number is greater than 1, and (4-1) = 3.

Example: Convert 0.05 to decimal notation.

Answer: 5×10^{-2}, since the five is two places behind the decimal (remember, the exponent is negative for numbers less than 1).

Any number raised to an exponent of zero is always 1. Also, unless you know what you're doing, always convert scientific notation to "regular" decimal numbers before doing arithmetic, and convert the answer back if necessary to answer the problem.

Area, Volume, and Surface Area

You can count on questions about area, volume, and surface area to be a significant part of the TABE. While commonly used formulas are provided in the actual TABE test book, it is best to become familiar with the formulas beforehand. A list is provided in the appendix for your convenience.

Percents

A percent can be converted to a decimal simply by dividing it by 100.

Example: What is 2% of 50?

Answer: 2% = 2/100 or .02, so .02 * 50 = 1

Word Problems

Percents

Example: Ticket sales for this year's annual concert at Minutemaid Park were $125,000. The promoter is predicting that next year's sales, in dollars, will be 40% greater than this year's. How many dollars in ticket sales is the promoter predicting for next year?

Answer: Next year's is 40% greater. 40% = 40/100 = .4, so .4 * $125,000 = $50,000. However, the example stated that next year's would be greater by that amount, so next year's sales would be this year's at $125,000 plus the increase at $50,000. $125,000 + $50,000 = $175,000

Distances

Example: In a certain triangle, the longest side is 1 foot longer than the second-longest side, and the second-longest side is 1 foot longer than the shortest side. If the perimeter is 30 feet, how many feet long is the shortest side.

Answer: There are three sides, let's call them A, B, and C. A is the longest, B the medium sized, and C the shortest. Because A is described in reference to B's length and B is described in reference to C's length, all calculations should be done off of C, the final reference. Use a variable to represent C's length, "x". This means that C is "x" long, B is "x + 1" because B was 1 foot longer than C, and A is "x + 1 + 1" because A was 1 foot longer than B. To calculate a perimeter you simply add all three sides together, so P = length A + length B + length C, or (x) + (x + 1) + (x + 1 +

- 9 -

1) = x + x + x + 1 + 1 + 1 = 3x + 3. You know that the perimeter equals 30 feet, so 3x + 3 = 30. Subtracting 3 from both sides gives 3x + 3 – 3 = 30 – 3 or 3x = 27. Dividing both sides by 3 to get "x" all by itself gives 3x / 3 = 27 / 3 or x = 9. So C = x = 9, and B = x + 1 = 9 + 1 = 10, and A = x + 1 + 1 = 9 + 1 + 1 = 11. A quick check of 9 + 10 + 11 = 30 for the perimeter distance proves that the answer of x = 9 is correct

Ratios

Example: An architect is drawing a scaled blueprint of an apartment building that is to be 100 feet wide and 250 feet long. On the drawing, if the building is 25 inches long, how many inches wide should it be?

Answer: Recognize the word "scaled" to indicate a similar drawing. Similar drawings or shapes can be solved using ratios. First, create the ratio fraction for the missing number, in this case the number of inches wide the drawing should be. The numerator of the first ratio fraction will be the matching known side, in this case "100 feet" wide. The question "100 feet wide is to how many inches wide?" gives us the first fraction of 100 / x. The question "250 feet long is to 25 inches long?" gives us the second fraction of 250 / 25. Again, note that both numerators (100 and 250) are from the same shape. The denominators ("x" and 25) are both from the same shape or drawing as well. Cross multiplication gives 100 * 25 = 250 * x or 2500 = 250x. Dividing both sides by 250 to get x by itself yields 2500 / 250 = 250x / 250 or 10 = x.

Special Formulas

FOIL (First, Outer, Inner, Last)

When you are given a problem such as (x + 2)(x – 3), you should use the FOIL method of multiplication. First, multiply the First parts of each equation (x*x). Then multiply the Outer parts of each equation (x*-3). Note that you should treat the minus 3 in the second equation as a negative 3. Then multiply the Inner parts of each equation (2*x). Finally, multiply the Last parts of each equation (2*-3). Once you are finished, add each part together (x*x)+(x*-3)+(2*x)+(2*-3) = x^2 + -3x + 2x + -6 = x^2 – 3x + 2x – 6 = x^2 – 1x –6 = x^2 – x – 6.

Slope-Intercept formula

$y = mx + b$, where m is the slope of the line and b is the y-intercept.

Example: In the (x,y) coordinate plane, what is the slope of the line $2y = x - 4$?

Answer: First this needs to be converted into slope intercept form. Divide both sides by 2, which gives $2y/2 = (x-4)/2$ or $y = x/2 - 2$. $x/2$ is the same as $\frac{1}{2}$ *x, so since m in the formula $y = mx+b$ is the slope, then in the equation $y = \frac{1}{2}$ * $x - 2$, $\frac{1}{2}$ is the slope.

Example: In the (x,y) coordinate plane, where does the line $y = 2x - 3$ cross the y-axis?

Answer: In the formula $y = mx + b$, b is the y – intercept, or where the line crosses the y-axis. In this case, b is represented by –3, so –3 is where the line crosses the y-axis.

Example: In the (x , y) coordinate plane, what is the slope of the line $y = x + 2$?

Answer: This is already in the slope intercept form of $y = mx + b$. Whenever x does not have a number in front of it, you can always assume that there is a 1 there. Therefore, this equation could also be written as $y = 1x + 2$, which means $m = 1$, and the slope is 1.

Slope formula

$m = (y1 - y2)/(x1 - x2)$, where m is the slope of the line and two points on the line are given by (x1,y1) and (x2,y2). This can sometimes be remembered by the statement "rise over run", which means that the "y" values represent the "rise" as they are the up and down dimension and the "x" values represent the "run" as they are the side to side dimension.

Example: What is the slope of a line that passes through points (5,1) and (-2, 3).

Answer: $m = (y1 - y2)/(x1 - x2)$ or $(1 - 3)/(5 - -2)$ or $-2 / (5 + 2)$ or $-2 / 7$

Line Plotting

If you are trying to plot a line, there is an easy way to do it. First convert the line into slope intercept form ($y = mx + b$). Then, put a dot on the y-axis at the value of b. For example, if you have a line given by $y = 2/3x + 1$, then the first point on the line would be at (0,1), because 1 is the y-intercept, or where the line crosses the y-axis. To find the next point on the line, use the slope, which is 2/3. First go 2 increments up, and then 3 increments to the right. To find the next point on the line, go 2 more increments up, and then 3 more increments to the right. You should always go either up or down depending on the numerator in the slope fraction. So if the slope is 3/5, then the numerator is 3, and you should go 3 increments up and 5 increments to the right.

- 11 -

You should always go to the right the amount of the denominator. So if the slope is –2, then first you should remember that –2 is the same as –2/1. Since –2 is the numerator, you should go down 2 increments and then 1 increment to the right.

Remember that positive slopes slope upward from left to right and that negative slopes slope downward from left to right.

Simple Probability

The probability problems on the TABE are fairly straightforward. The basic idea is this: the probability that something will happen is the number of possible ways that something can happen divided by the total number of possible ways for all things that can happen.

Example: I have 20 balloons, 12 are red, 8 are yellow. I give away one yellow balloon; if the next balloon is randomly picked, what is the probability that it will be yellow?

Answer: The probability is 7/19, because after giving one away, there are 7 different ways that the "something" can happen, divided by 19 remaining possibilities.

Ratios

When a question asks about two similar shapes, expect a ratio problem.

Example: The figure below shows 2 triangles, where triangle ABC ~ A'B'C'. In these similar triangles, a = 3, b = 4, c = 5, and a' = 6. What is the value of b'?

Answer: You are given the dimensions of 1 side that is similar on both triangles (a and a'). You are looking for b' and are given the dimensions of b. Therefore you can set up a ratio of a/a' = b/b' or 3/6 = 4/b'. To solve, cross multiply the two sides, multiplying 6*4 = 3*b' or 24 = 3b'. Dividing both sides by 3 (24/3 = 3b'/3) makes 8 = b', so 8 is the answer.

Note many other problems may have opportunities to use a ratio. Look for problems where you are trying to find dimensions for a shape and you have dimensions for a similar shape. These can nearly always be solved by setting up a ratio. Just be careful and set up corresponding measurements in the ratios. First decide what you are being asked for on shape B, represented by a variable, such as x. Then ask yourself, which side on similar shape A is the same size side as x. That is your first ratio fraction, set up a fraction like 2/x if 2 is the similar size side on shape A. Then find a side on each shape that is similar. If 4 is the size of another side on shape A and it corresponds to a side with size 3 on shape B, then your second ratio fraction is 4/3. Note that 2 and 4 are the two numerators in the ratio fractions and are both from shape A. Also note that "x" the unknown side and 3 are both the denominators in the ratio fractions and are both from shape B.

Graphs

Midpoints

To find a midpoint, find the difference in the x-direction between the two endpoints given, and divide by two. Then add that number to the leftmost endpoint's x coordinate. That will be the x coordinate of the midpoint. Next find the difference in the y-direction between the two endpoints given, and divide by two. Then add that number to the lower endpoint's y coordinate. That will be the y coordinate of the midpoint.

Example: What is the midpoint of the line segment with endpoints of (-2 , 5) and (4 , 1)?

Answer: First, subtract the leftmost endpoint's x coordinate from the rightmost endpoint's x coordinate 4 - -2 = 4 + 2 = 6. Then divide by two, 6 / 2 = 3. Then add that number to the leftmost x coordinate -2 + 3 = 1, which is the midpoint's x coordinate. Second, subtract the lower endpoint's y coordinate from the higher endpoint's y coordinate 5 − 1 = 4. Then divide by two, 4 / 2 = 2. Then add that number to the lower y coordinate 1 + 2 = 3, which is the midpoint's y coordinate. So the midpoint is given by (1 , 3).

Angles

If you have a two intersecting lines, remember that the sum of all of the angles can only be 360°. In fact, the two angles on either side of each line will add up to 180°. In the example below, on either side of each line, there is a 137° angle and a 43° angle (137° + 43°) = 180°. Also note that opposite angles are equal. For example, the 43° angle is matched by a similar 43° angle on the opposite side of the intersection.

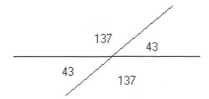

Additionally, parallel lines intersected by a third line will share angles. In the example below, note how each 128° angle is matched by a 128° angle on the opposite side. Also, all of the other angles in this example are 52° angles, because all of the angles on one side of a line have to equal 180° and since there are only two angles, if you have the degree of one, then you can find the degree of the other. In this case, the missing angle is given by 180° − 128° = 52°.

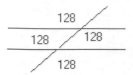

Finally, remember that all of the angles in a triangle will add up to 180°. If you are given two of the angles, then subtract them both from 180° and you will have the degree of the third missing angle.

Example: If you have a triangle with two given angles of 20° and 130°, what degree is the third angle?

Answer: All angles must add up to 180°, so 180° − 20° − 130° = 30°.

Right Triangles

Whenever you see the words "right triangle" or "90° angle," alarm bells should go off. These problems will almost always involve the law of right triangles, AKA The Pythagorean Theorem:

$A^2 + B^2 = C^2$

Where A = the length of one of the shorter sides

B = the length of the other shorter side

C = the length of the hypotenuse or longest side opposite the 90° angle

MAKE SURE YOU KNOW THIS FORMULA. At least 3-5 questions will reference variations on this formula by giving you two of the three variables and asking you to solve for the third.

Example: A right triangle has sides of 3 and 4; what is the length of the hypotenuse?

Answer: Solving the equation, $A^2=9$, $B^2=16$, so $C^2=25$; the square root of 25 is 5, the length of the hypotenuse C.

Example: In the rectangle below, what is the length of the diagonal line?

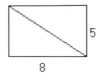

Answer: This rectangle is actually made of two right triangles. Whenever you have a right triangle, the Pythagorean Theorem can be used. Since the right side of the triangle is equal to 5, then the left side must also be equal to 5. This creates a triangle with one side equal to 5 and another side equal to 8. To use the Pythagorean Theorem, we state that $5^2 + 8^2 = C^2$ or $25 + 64 = C^2$ or $89 = C^2$ or C = Square Root of 89

Circles

Many test takers have never seen the formula for a circle:

$(x-A)^2 + (y-B)^2 = r^2$

This looks intimidating, but it's really not:

A = the coordinate of the center on the x-axis

B = the coordinate of the center on the y-axis

r = the radius of the circle

Example: What is the radius of the circle described by: $(x+2)^2 + (x-3)^2 = 16$

Answer: Since $r^2 = 16$, r, the radius, equals 4.

Also, this circle is centered at (-2,3) since those must be the values of A and B in the generic equation to make it the same as this equation.

Final Note

As mentioned before, word problems describing shapes should always be drawn out. Remember the old adage that a picture is worth a thousand words. If geometric shapes are described (line segments, circles, squares, etc) draw them out rather than trying to visualize how they should look.

Approach problems systematically. Take time to understand what is being asked for. In many cases there is a drawing or graph that you can write on. Draw lines, jot notes, do whatever is necessary to create a visual picture and to allow you to understand what is being asked.

Even if you have always done well in math, you may not succeed on the TABE. While normal math tests in school test specific competencies in specific subjects, the TABE frequently tests your ability to apply math concepts from vastly different math subjects in one problem. However, in few cases is any TABE Mathematics problem more than two "layers" deep.

What does this mean for you? You can easily learn the TABE Mathematics through taking multiple practice tests. If you have some gaps in your math knowledge, we suggest you buy a more basic study guide to help you build a foundation before applying our secrets.

English Section

Skimming

Your first task when you begin reading a passage is to answer the question "What is the topic of the selection?" This can best be answered by quickly skimming the passage for the general idea, stopping to read only the first sentence of each paragraph. A paragraph's first sentence is usually the main topic sentence, and it gives you a summary of the content of the paragraph.

Once you've skimmed the passage, stopping to read only the first sentences, you will have a general idea about what it is about, as well as what is the expected topic in each paragraph.

Each question will contain clues as to where to find the answer in the passage. Do not just randomly search through the passage for the correct answer to each question. Search scientifically. Find key word(s) or ideas in the question that are going to either contain or be near the correct answer. These are typically nouns, verbs, numbers, or phrases in the question that will probably be duplicated in the passage. Once you have identified those key word(s) or idea, skim the passage quickly to find where those key word(s) or idea appears. The correct answer choice will be nearby.

Example: What caused Martin to suddenly return to Paris?

The key word is Paris. Skim the passage quickly to find where this word appears. The answer will be close by that word.

However, sometimes key words in the question are not repeated in the passage. In those cases, search for the general idea of the question.

Example: Which of the following was the psychological impact of the author's childhood upon the remainder of his life?

-18-

Key words are "childhood" or "psychology". While searching for those words, be alert for other words or phrases that have similar meaning, such as "emotional effect" or "mentally" which could be used in the passage, rather than the exact word "psychology".

Numbers or years can be particularly good key words to skim for, as they stand out from the rest of the text.

Example: Which of the following best describes the influence of Monet's work in the 20th century?

20th contains numbers and will easily stand out from the rest of the text. Use 20th as the key word to skim for in the passage.

Other good key word(s) may be in quotation marks. These identify a word or phrase that is copied directly from the passage. In those cases, the word(s) in quotation marks are exactly duplicated in the passage.

Example: In her college years, what was meant by Margaret's "drive for excellence"?

"Drive for excellence" is a direct quote from the passage and should be easy to find.

Once you've quickly found the correct section of the passage to find the answer, focus upon the answer choices. Sometimes a choice will repeat word for word a portion of the passage near the answer. However, beware of such duplication – it may be a trap! More than likely, the correct choice will paraphrase or summarize the related portion of the passage, rather than being exactly the same wording.

For the answers that you think are correct, read them carefully and make sure that they answer the question. An answer can be factually correct, but it MUST answer the question asked. Additionally, two answers can both be seemingly correct, so be sure to read all of the answer choices, and make sure that you get the one that BEST answers the question.

Some questions will not have a key word.

Example: Which of the following would the author of this passage likely agree with?

In these cases, look for key words in the answer choices. Then skim the passage to find where the answer choice occurs. By skimming to find where to look, you can minimize the time required.

Sometimes it may be difficult to identify a good key word in the question to skim for in the passage. In those cases, look for a key word in one of the answer choices to skim for. Often the answer choices can all be found in the same paragraph, which can quickly narrow your search.

Paragraph Focus

Focus upon the first sentence of each paragraph, which is the most important. The main topic of the paragraph is usually there.

Once you've read the first sentence in the paragraph, you have a general idea about what each paragraph will be about. As you read the questions, try to determine which paragraph will have the answer. Paragraphs have a concise topic. The answer should either obviously be there or obviously not. It will save time if you can jump straight to the paragraph, so try to remember what you learned from the first sentences.

Example: The first paragraph is about poets; the second is about poetry. If a question asks about poetry, where will the answer be? The second paragraph.

The main idea of a passage is typically spread across all or most of its paragraphs. Whereas the main idea of a paragraph may be completely different than the main idea of the very next paragraph, a main idea for a passage affects all of the paragraphs in one form or another.

Example: What is the main idea of the passage?

For each answer choice, try to see how many paragraphs are related. It can help to count how many sentences are affected by each choice, but it is best to see how many paragraphs are affected by the choice. Typically the answer choices will include incorrect choices that are main ideas of individual paragraphs, but not the entire passage. That is why it is crucial to choose ideas that are supported by the most paragraphs possible.

Eliminate Choices

Some choices can quickly be eliminated. "Andy Warhol lived there." Is Andy Warhol even mentioned in the article? If not, quickly eliminate it.

When trying to answer a question such as "the passage indicates all of the following EXCEPT" quickly skim the paragraph searching for references to each choice. If the reference exists, scratch it off as a choice. Similar choices may be crossed off simultaneously if they are close enough.

In choices that ask you to choose "which answer choice does NOT describe?" or "all of the following answer choices are identifiable characteristics, EXCEPT which?" look for answers that are similarly worded. Since only one answer can be correct, if there are two answers that appear to mean the same thing, they must BOTH be incorrect, and can be eliminated.

Example:

A.   changing values and attitudes

B.   a large population of mobile or uprooted people

These answer choices are similar; they both describe a fluid culture. Because of their similarity, they can be linked together. Since the answer can have only one choice, they can also be eliminated together.

When presented with a question that offers two choices, or neither choice, or both choice, it is rarely both choices.

Example: When an atom emits a beta particle, the mass of the atom will:

A.   increase

B.   decrease.

C.   stay the same.

D.   either increase or decrease depending on conditions.

Answer D will rarely be correct, the answers are usually more concrete.

Contextual Clues

Look for contextual clues. An answer can be right but not correct. The contextual clues will help you find the answer that is most right and is correct. Understand the context in which a phrase is stated.

When asked for the implied meaning of a statement made in the passage, immediately go find the statement and read the context it was made in. Also, look for an answer choice that has a similar phrase to the statement in question.

Example: In the passage, what is implied by the phrase "Churches have become more or less part of the furniture"?

Find an answer choice that is similar or describes the phrase "part of the furniture" as that is the key phrase in the question. "Part of the furniture" is a saying that means something is fixed, immovable, or set in their ways. Those are all similar ways of saying "part of the furniture." As such, the correct answer choice will probably include a similar rewording of the expression.

Example: Why was John described as "morally desperate".

The answer will probably have some sort of definition of morals in it. "Morals" refers to a code of right and wrong behavior, so the correct answer choice will likely have words that mean something like that.

Fact/Opinion

When asked about which statement is a fact or opinion, remember that answer choices that are facts will typically have no ambiguous words. For example, how long is a long time? What defines an ordinary person? These ambiguous words of "long" and "ordinary" should not be in a factual statement. However, if all of the choices have ambiguous words, go to the context of the passage. Often a factual statement may be set out as a research finding.

Example: "The scientist found that the eye reacts quickly to change in light."

Opinions may be set out in the context of words like thought, believed, understood, or wished.

Example: "He thought the Yankees should win the World Series."

Opposites

Answer choices that are direct opposites are usually correct. The paragraph will often contain established relationships (when this goes up, that goes down). The question may ask you to draw conclusions for this and will give two similar answer choices that are opposites.

Example:

A. if other factors are held constant, then increasing the interest rate will lead to a decrease in housing starts

B. if other factors are held constant, then increasing the interest rate will lead to an increase in housing starts

Often these opposites will not be so clearly recognized. Don't be thrown off by different wording, look for the meaning beneath. Notice how these two answer choices are really opposites, with just a slight change in the wording shown above. Once you realize these are opposites, you should examine them closely. One of these two is likely to be the correct answer.

Example:

A. if other factors are held constant, then increasing the interest rate will lead to a decrease in housing starts

B. when there is an increase in housing starts, and other things remaining equal, it is often the result of an increase in interest rates

Make Predictions

As you read and understand the passage and then the question, try to guess what the answer will be. Remember that four of the five answer choices are wrong, and once you being reading them, your mind will immediately become cluttered with answer choices designed to throw you off. Your mind is typically the most focused immediately after you have read the passage and question and digested its contents. If you can, try to predict what the correct answer will be. You may be surprised at what you can predict.

Quickly scan the choices and see if your prediction is in the listed answer choices. If it is, then you can be quite confident that you have the right answer. It still won't hurt to check the other answer choices, but most of the time, you've got it!

Answer the Question

It may seem obvious to only pick answer choices that answer the question, but TABE can create some excellent answer choices that are wrong. Don't pick an answer just because it sounds right, or you believe it to be true. It MUST answer the question. Once you've made your selection, always go back and check it against the question and make sure that you didn't misread the question, and the answer choice does answer the question posed.

Benchmark

After you read the first answer choice, decide if you think it sounds correct or not. If it doesn't, move on to the next answer choice. If it does, make a mental note about that choice. This doesn't mean that you've definitely selected it as your answer choice, it just means that it's the best you've seen thus far. Go ahead and read the next choice. If the next choice is worse than the one you've already selected, keep going to the next answer choice. If the next choice is better than the choice you've already selected, then make a mental note about that answer choice.

As you read through the list, you are mentally noting the choice you think is right. That is your new standard. Every other answer choice must be benchmarked against that standard. That choice is correct until proven otherwise by another answer choice beating it out. Once you've decided that no other answer choice seems as good, do one final check to ensure that it answers the question posed.

New Information

Correct answers will usually contain the information listed in the paragraph and question. Rarely will completely new information be inserted into a correct answer choice. Occasionally the new information may be related in a manner that TABE is asking for you to interpret, but seldom.

Example:

The argument above is dependent upon which of the following assumptions?

A. Scientists have used Charles's Law to interpret the relationship.

If Charles's Law is not mentioned at all in the referenced paragraph and argument, then it is unlikely that this choice is correct. All of the information needed to answer the question is provided for you, and so you should not have to make guesses that are unsupported or choose answer choices that have unknown information that cannot be reasoned.

Key Words

Look for answer choices that have the same key words in them as the question.

Example:

Which of the following, if true, would best explain the reluctance of politicians since 1980 to support this funding?

Look for the key words "since 1980" to be referenced in the correct answer choice. Most valid answer choices would probably include a phrase such as "since 1980, politicians have..."

Valid Information

Don't discount any of the information provided in the passage, particularly shorter ones. Every piece of information may be necessary to determine the correct answer. None of the information

- 25 -

in the paragraph is there to throw you off (while the answer choices will certainly have information to throw you off). If two seemingly unrelated topics are discussed, don't ignore either. You can be confident there is a relationship, or it wouldn't be included in the paragraph, and you are probably going to have to determine what is that relationship for the answer.

Time Management

In technical passages, do not get lost on the technical terms. Skip them and move on. You want a general understanding of what is going on, not a mastery of the passage.

When you encounter material in the selection that seems difficult to understand, it often may not be necessary and can be skipped. Only spend time trying to understand it if it is going to be relevant for a question. Understand difficult phrases only as a last resort.

Answer general questions before detail questions. A reader with a good understanding of the whole passage can often answer general questions without rereading a word. Get the easier questions out of the way before tackling the more time consuming ones.

Identify each question by type. Usually the wording of a question will tell you whether you can find the answer by referring directly to the passage or by using your reasoning powers. You alone know which question types you customarily handle with ease and which give you trouble and will require more time. Save the difficult questions for last.

Final Warnings

Hedge Phrases Revisited

Once again, watch out for critical "hedge" phrases, such as likely, may, can, will often, sometimes, etc, often, almost, mostly, usually, generally, rarely, sometimes. Question writers insert these hedge phrases, to cover every possibility. Often an answer will be wrong simply because it leaves no room for exception.

Example: Animals live longer in cold places than animals in warm places.

This answer choice is wrong, because there are exceptions in which certain warm climate animals live longer. This answer choice leaves no possibility of exception. It states that every animal species in cold places live longer than animal species in warm places. Correct answer choices will typically have a key hedge word to leave room for exceptions.

Example: In severe cold, a polar bear cub is likely to survive longer than an adult polar bear.

This answer choice is correct, because not only does the passage imply that younger animals survive better in the cold, it also allows for exceptions to exist. The use of the word "likely" leaves room for cases in which a polar bear cub might not survive longer than the adult polar bear.

Word Usage Questions

When asked how a word is used in the passage, don't use your existing knowledge of the word. The question is being asked precisely because there is some strange or unusual usage of the word in the passage. Go to the passage and use contextual clues to determine the answer. Don't simply use the popular definition you already know.

Switchback Words

Stay alert for "switchbacks". These are the words and phrases frequently used to alert you to shifts in thought. The most common switchback word is "but". Others include although, however, nevertheless, on the other hand, even though, while, in spite of, despite, regardless of.

Avoid "Fact Traps"

Once you know which paragraph the answer will be in, focus on that paragraph. However, don't get distracted by a choice that is factually true about the paragraph. Your search is for the answer that answers the question, which may be about a tiny aspect in the paragraph. Stay focused and don't fall for an answer that describes the larger picture of the paragraph. Always go back to the question and make sure you're choosing an answer that actually answers the question and is not just a true statement.

Word Confusion

"Which" should be used to refer to things only.

John's dog, which was called Max, is large and fierce.

"That" may be used to refer to either persons or things.

Is this the only book that Louis L'Amour wrote?

Is Louis L'Amour the author that [or who] wrote Western novels?

"Who" should be used to refer to persons only.

Mozart was the composer who [or that] wrote those operas.

Correct pronoun usage in combinations

To determine the correct pronoun form in a compound subject, try each subject separately with the verb, adapting the form as necessary. Your ear will tell you which form is correct.

Example: Bob and (I, me) will be going.

Restate the sentence twice, using each subject individually. Bob will be going. I will be going. "Me will be going" does not make sense.

When a pronoun is used with a noun immediately following (as in "we boys"), say the sentence without the added noun. Your ear will tell you the correct pronoun form.

Example: (We/Us) boys played football last year.

Restate the sentence twice, without the noun. We played football last year. Us played football last year. Clearly "We played football last year" makes more sense.

Commas

Flow

Commas break the flow of text. To test whether they are necessary, while reading the text to yourself, pause for a moment at each comma. If the pauses seem natural, then the commas are correct. If they are not, then the commas are not correct.

Nonessential clauses and phrases

A comma should be used to set off nonessential clauses and nonessential participial phrases from the rest of the sentence. To determine if a clause is essential, remove it from the sentence. If the removal of the clause would alter the meaning of the sentence, then it is essential. Otherwise, it is nonessential.

Example: John Smith, who was a disciple of Andrew Collins, was a noted archeologist.
In the example above, the sentence describes John Smith's fame in archeology. The fact that he was a disciple of Andrew Collins is not necessary to that meaning. Therefore, separating it from the rest of the sentence with commas, is correct.

Do not use a comma if the clause or phrase is essential to the meaning of the sentence.
Example: Anyone who appreciates obscure French poetry will enjoy reading the book.

If the phrase "who appreciates obscure French poetry" is removed, the sentence would indicate that anyone would enjoy reading the book, not just those with an appreciation for obscure French poetry. However, the sentence implies that the book's enjoyment may not be for everyone, so the phrase is essential.

Another perhaps easier way to determine if the clause is essential is to see if it has a comma at its beginning or end. Consistent, parallel punctuation must be used, and so if you can determine a comma exists at one side of the clause, then you can be certain that a comma should exist on the opposite side.

Independent clauses

Use a comma before the words and, but, or, nor, for, yet when they join independent clauses. To determine if two clauses are independent, remove the word that joins them. If the two clauses are capable of being their own sentence by themselves, then they are independent and need a comma between them.
Example: He ran down the street, and then he ran over the bridge.

He ran down the street. Then he ran over the bridge. These are both clauses capable of being their own sentence. Therefore a comma must be used along with the word "and" to join the two clauses together.

If one or more of the clauses would be a fragment if left alone, then it must be joined to another clause and does not need a comma between them.
Example: He ran down the street and over the bridge.

He ran down the street. Over the bridge. "Over the bridge" is a sentence fragment and is not capable of existing on its own. No comma is necessary to join it with "He ran down the street".

Note that this does not cover the use of "and" when separating items in a series, such as "red, white, and blue". In these cases a comma is not always necessary between the last two items in the series, but in general it is best to use one.

Parenthetical expressions
Commas should separate parenthetical expressions such as the following: after all, by the way, for example, in fact, on the other hand.
Example: By the way, she is in my biology class.

If the parenthetical expression is in the middle of the sentence, a comma would be both before and after it.
Example: She is, after all, in my biology class.

However, these expressions are not always used parenthetically. In these cases, commas are not used. To determine if an expression is parenthetical, see if it would need a pause if you were reading the text. If it does, then it is parenthetical and needs commas.

Example: You can tell by the way she plays the violin that she enjoys its music.

No pause is necessary in reading that example sentence. Therefore the phrase "by the way" does not need commas around it.

Hyphens

Hyphenate a compound adjective that is directly before the noun it describes.

Example 1: He was the best-known kid in the school.

Example 2: The shot came from that grass-covered hill.

Example 3: The well-drained fields were dry soon after the rain.

Semicolons

Period replacement

A semicolon is often described as either a weak period or strong comma. Semicolons should separate independent clauses that could stand alone as separate sentences. To test where a semicolon should go, replace it with a period in your mind. If the two independent clauses would seem normal with the period, then the semicolon is in the right place.

Example: The rain had finally stopped; a few rays of sunshine were pushing their way through the clouds.

The rain had finally stopped. A few rays of sunshine were pushing their way through the clouds. These two sentences can exist independently with a period between them. Because they are also closely related in thought, a semicolon is a good choice to combine them.

Transitions

When a semicolon is next to a transition word, such as "however", it comes before the word.

Example: The man in the red shirt stood next to her; however, he did not know her name.

If these two clauses were separated with a period, the period would go before the word "however" creating the following two sentences: The man in the red shirt stood next to her. However, he did not know her name. The semicolon can function as a weak period and join the two clauses by replacing the period.

Sentence Correction

These questions will test your ability of correct and effective expression. Choose your answer carefully, utilizing the standards of written English, including grammar rules, the proper choice of words and of sentence construction. The correct answer will flow smoothly and be both clear and concise.

Use Your Ear

Read each sentence carefully, inserting the answer choices as replacements for the section of the sentence being asked about. Don't stop at the first answer choice if you think it is right, but read them all. What may seem like the best choice, at first, may not be after you have had time to read all of the choices. Allow your ear to determine what sounds right. Often one or two answer choices can be immediately ruled out because it doesn't make sound logical or make sense.

Contextual Clues

It bears repeating that contextual clues offer a lot of help in determining the best answer. Key words in the sentence will allow you to determine exactly which answer choice is the best replacement text.

Example:

Archeology has shown that some of the ruins of the ancient city of Babylon are approximately 500 years <u>as old as any supposed</u> Mesopotamian predecessors.

A.) as old as their supposed

B.) older than their supposed

In this example, the key word "supposed" is used. Archaeology would either confirm that the predecessors to Babylon were more ancient or disprove that supposition. Since supposed was used, it would imply that archaeology had disproved the accepted belief, making Babylon actually older, not as old as, and answer choice "B" correct.

Furthermore, because "500 years" is used, answer choice A can be ruled out. Years are used to show either absolute or relative age. If two objects are as old as each other, no years are necessary to describe that relationship, and it would be sufficient to say, "The ancient city of Babylon is approximately as old as their supposed Mesopotamian predecessors," without using the term "500 years".

Simplicity is Bliss

Simplicity cannot be overstated. You should never choose a longer, more complicated, or wordier replacement if a simple one will do. When a point can be made with fewer words, choose that answer. However, never sacrifice the flow of text for simplicity. If an answer is simple, but does not make sense, then it is not correct.

Beware of added phrases that don't add anything of meaning, such as "to be" or "as to them". Often these added phrases will occur just before a colon, which may come before a list of items. However, the colon does not need a lengthy introduction. The italics phrases in the below examples are wordy and unnecessary. They should be removed and the colon placed directly after the words "sport" and "following".

Example 1: There are many advantages to running as a sport, *of which the top advantages are*:
Example 2: The school supplies necessary were the following, *of which a few are*:

Punctuation

If a section of text has an opening dash, parentheses, or comma at the beginning of a phrase, then you can be sure there should be a matching closing dash, parentheses, or comma at the end of the phrase. If items in a series all have commas between them, then any additional items in that series will also gain commas. Do not alternate punctuation. If a dash is at the beginning of a statement, then do not put a parenthesis at the ending of the statement.

Sentence Completions

Read each sentence, inserting the answer choices in the blanks. Don't stop at the first answer choice if you think it is right, but read them all. What may seem like the best choice, at first, may not be after you have had time to read all of the choices.

Adjectives Give it Away

Words mean things and are added to the sentence for a reason. Adjectives in particular may be the clue to determining which answer choice is correct.

Example:

The brilliant scientist made several _____ discoveries.

    A. dull

    B. dazzling

Look at the adjectives first to help determine what makes sense. A "brilliant" or smart scientist would make dazzling, rather than dull discoveries. Without that simple adjective, no answer choice is clear.

Use Logic

Ask yourself questions about each answer choice to see if they are logical.

Example:

The deep pounding resonance of the drums could be ____ far off in the distance.

    A. seen

    B. heard

Would resonating poundings be "seen"? or Would resonating pounding be "heard"?

Multiple Blanks Are an Opportunity

Some sentence completion questions may have multiple blanks. It may be easier to focus on only one of the blanks and try to determine which answer choices could logically fit. This may allow you to eliminate some of the answer choices and concentrate only upon the ones that remain.

Transitional Words

Watch out for key transitional words! This can include however, but, yet, although, so, because, etc. These may change the meaning of a sentence and the context of the missing word.

- 34

Example:

He is an excellent marksman, but surprisingly, he _____ comes home empty handed from a hunting trip.

    A. often

    B. never

    C. rarely

A good shot or marksman would be expected to be a successful hunter. Watch out though for the transition phrase "but surprisingly". It indicates the opposite of what you would expect, which means this particular marksman must not be a successful hunter. A successful hunter would either never or rarely come home empty handed from a hunt, but an unsuccessful hunter would "often" come home empty handed, making "a" the correct answer.

The Trap of Familiarity

Don't just choose a word because you recognize it. On difficult questions, you may only recognize one or two words. TABE doesn't put "make-believe words" on the test, so don't think that just because you only recognize one word means that word must be correct. If you don't recognize four words, then focus on the one that you do recognize. Is it correct? Try your best to determine if it fits the sentence. If it does, that is great, but if it doesn't, eliminate it.

Practice Tests

Language Practice Questions

For Questions 1-3, select the correct punctuation mark for the sentence.

1. I knew the price of housing was going to increase but I had no idea that it would go up so much!
    a. ;
    b. :
    c. ,
    d. None

2. As a matter of fact everything she said was true.
    a. ;
    b. –
    c. ,
    d. None

3. Michael had been studying for this exam for two weeks but still could not pass.
    a. ;
    b. :
    c. ,
    d. None

For Questions 4-6, choose the best word or phrase to complete the sentence.

4. This tree _____ a lot since I started watering it more.
    a. grew
    b. is growing
    c. has grown
    d. grows

5. Barney did really _____ and finished in the top three in the competition.
    a. excellent
    b. well
    c. good
    d. fine

6. My mother gave the tickets to my brother and ____.
    a. I
    b. they
    c. she
    d. me

For Questions 7-17, select the complete sentence that is written correctly.

7.
    a. A group of six people are affected.
    b. This box of papers belong in the desk
    c. A collection of stamps is selling for a dollar.
    d. Two hundred cars, every hour, cross the bridge.

8.
    a. The water is fall to the ground.
    b. She and her mother went to church.
    c. The sheriff were waiting for them.
    d. Not, another word out of you.

9.
    a. He applied for a loan.
    b. One of a kind.
    c. They struggled, for nearly an hour.
    d. Coming out of the country.

10.
    a. Renting a movie is less fun than the excitement of being there.
    b. Her native language, French was easier for her to speak than English.
    c. In a challenging environment, she found the best in herself.
    d. We went shopping for a new camera, most were digital models.

11.
    a. Here today gone tomorrow
    b. It wouldn't have happened if I hadn't went there.
    c. A stitch in time, saves nine.
    d. Give me a dollar.

12.
    a. Not an option.
    b. Holiday shopping.
    c. Can you open this for me, please?
    d. This one is mine, that one is her's.

13.
    a. It's no wonder that his friends nicknamed him Goth.
    b. He ain't done nothing but sleep.
    c. He was a habitual scoundrel; one who would beat the check in restaurants.
    d. Cold soup don't taste good.

14.
    a. The plaintiff, who plans to appeal appeared unfazed.
    b. She'll get paid, I hope, within a few weeks.
    c. Of the three she was the tallest.
    d. I couldn't hardly wait for the sequel.

15.
   a. Do you know the poem "Wait Until Later?"
   b. "Of all the stories in this book," she said, "this is my favorite."
   c. Jack mentioned the poem Ode to a Nightingale in his letter.
   d. Mike's father asked him "what was wrong."

16.
   a. In the local currency yen everything seemed to be more expensive.
   b. My new car a Honda.
   c. I don't understand why she keeps calling me?
   d. Is there anyone here with change of a dollar?

17.
   a. Got a couple of friends to help me.
   b. "Canada" is a country in North America.
   c. She was feeling weak and almost fainted.
   d. When boating I always wear a life vest.

For Questions 18-21, select the answer that best combines the underlined sentences into one.

18. I spent $25,000 on a new car.
   I don't have enough money left for maintenance.
   a. After spending $25,000 on a new car, I don't have enough money left for maintenance.
   b. I spent $25,000 on a new car because I don't have enough money left for maintenance.
   c. I spent $25,000 on a new car when I don't have enough money left for maintenance.
   d. When I spent $25,000 on a new car I don't have enough money left for maintenance.

19. She was the first female president of the company.
   Her success met with derision from many people in the community.
   a. When her success met with derision from many people in the community, she was the first female president of the company.
   b. She was the first female president of the company, but her success met with derision from many people in the community.
   c. She was the first female president of the company, whenever her success met with derision from many people in the community.
   d. She was the first female president of the company whose success met with derision from many people in the community

20. The center fielder broke the season record for home runs.
   He was handsomely rewarded.
   a. The handsome center fielder was rewarded for breaking the season record for home runs.
   b. The center fielder was handsomely rewarded, breaking the season record for home runs.
   c. The center fielder was handsomely rewarded for breaking the season record for home runs.
   d. The handsomely rewarded center fielder broke the season record for home runs.

21. The mechanic performed a number of diagnostic tests on the car.
    The mechanic used a computer to perform the diagnostic tests.
    a. While performing a number of diagnostic tests on the car, the mechanic used a computer to perform the tests.
    b. Although the mechanic used a computer, he performed a number of diagnostic tests on the car.
    c. Because he used a computer, the mechanic performed a number of diagnostic tests on the car.
    d. The mechanic used a computer to perform a number of diagnostic tests on the car.

For Questions 22-27, choose the best sentence to fill in the blank in the paragraph.

22. _____. This letter tells the employer why you are qualified for the job you are applying for. Effective application letters explain the reasons for your interest in the specific organization and identify your most relevant skills or experiences.
    a. A letter of application should be sent with your resume to provide additional information.
    b. It is not enough merely to send a resume in with your job application.
    c. The resume and letter of application demonstrate your qualifications to prospective employers.
    d. When applying for a job, always request a personal interview.

23. _____. Books may be thrown from shelving. Roofs, rooms and buildings may collapse, burying collections under furniture, beams, dirt and debris, or leaving collections exposed and vulnerable to wind, rain and snow. Structural collapse may cause broken gas and power lines, leading to fire damage to collections as well as water damage from fire hoses and sprinklers.
    a. People are frequently killed by earthquakes.
    b. The Loma Prieta earthquake did a lot of damage to libraries and their collections.
    c. Earthquakes can damage library collections in many ways.
    d. Never go into a library during an earthquake.

24. Sunscreens are lotions that help prevent the sun's ultraviolet rays from reaching the skin. _____. UVB is the main cause of sunburn, whereas the more penetrating UVA rays are the cause of wrinkling and sagging of the skin. They also add to the carcinogenic effects of UVB rays. Sunscreens vary in their ability to protect against UVA and UVB.
    a. You can get a sunburn on cloudy days as well as on sunny ones.
    b. There are two types of ultraviolet radiation, UVA and UVB, that damage skin and increase the risk of skin cancer.
    c. The sun is particularly damaging at high altitudes.
    d. A day without coffee is like a day without sunshine.

25. Most banks offer checking accounts for their customers. Usually, they require an initial deposit before establishing a new account, along with identification and proof of address. You may opt for a no-frills checking account, which doesn't charge fees, or choose one that pays interest but requires maintaining a high minimum balance. _____.
    a. A bank is an institution that provides financial services to its customers.
    b. Banks are licensed by the government.
    c. There may also be surcharges for ATM usage and other services.
    d. Banking is a rewarding profession.

26. The Florida Everglades cover thousands of square miles between the east and west coasts of Florida. Everglades National Park is the centerpiece of the region, but there are other great places to explore. _____. The weather is mild, birds are abundant, and there are fewer mosquitoes than at other times of year.
  a. The best time to visit is during the winter, from November through early April.
  b. The park is run by the National Parks Service.
  c. Many visitors come to see the alligators.
  d. One way to see the Everglades is by boat.

27. Organic food standards are defined by a 2002 federal law. _____. Use of pesticides and other synthetic chemicals is forbidden. As a result of this law, wherever you go in the fifty states you can be certain that produce carrying an organic label was grown in accordance with the same standards. That fact has helped increase organic food sales.
  a. You can now buy organic foods at most markets.
  b. Many other laws were passed in 2002.
  c. Organic foods are sometimes more expensive.
  d. It outlines how products must be grown in order to be certified organic.

For Questions 28 and 29, choose the best sentence to follow and develop the topic sentence that is given.

28. Tooth enamel is the hardest part of the human body.
  a. Most people have 32 teeth.
  b. It is made almost entirely of minerals, with a small amount of organic material.
  c. Dentures, bridges and fillings are common dental appliances.
  d. You should visit your dentist regularly to take care of you teeth.

29. More than 200 people were rescued after an Egyptian ferry sank in the Red Sea.
  a. The Red Sea is a popular tourist destination in the Middle East.
  b. Egypt is the most populous country in North Africa.
  c. Authorities blamed rough seas and overloading of the ferry.
  d. January is the coldest month in these waters.

For questions 30 and 31, select the sentence that does not belong in the paragraph.

30. In 1957 Fortune magazine ran an article about Jean Paul Getty. (A) It suggested that Getty was the richest man in the world. (B) A museum is built on his estate today. (C) An interviewer asked Getty how much he thought he could really get in cash if he were to sell his oil, realty, art and other holdings. (D) A note of gone-are-the-better-days crept into his response. "I would hope to realize several billions," he said. "But, remember, a billion dollars isn't worth what it used to be."
  a.
  b.
  c.
  d.

31. (A) Vegetable oil can be used in as fuel in diesel-powered automobiles. (B) There are almost 250 million automobiles in the U.S. (C) It can even be used as is, without being converted to biodiesel. (D) The difficulty is that straight vegetable oil is much more viscous than conventional diesel fuel or biodiesel: studies have found that it can damage engines. But it can be used if you get a professional engine conversion.

    a.
    b.
    c.
    d.

For Questions 32-54, read the passage and select the correctly written answer to replace each underlined sentence or phrase.

Passage I

Settlement of Costa Rica began in 1522. For nearly three centuries, Spain administered the region under a military governor. The Spanish optimistically called the country "Rich Coast." **32.** Although they found little gold or other valuable minerals in Costa Rica, however, the Spanish turned to agriculture.

33. An equalness tradition arose in Costa Rica during the early years of Spanish colonization. This tradition survived the widened class distinctions brought on by the 19th-century introduction of banana and coffee cultivation and consequent accumulations of local wealth.

Costa Rica joined other Central American provinces in 1821 in a joint declaration of independence from Spain. **34.** The newly independent provinces formed a federation when border disputes broke out among them. **35.** Costa Rica's northern Guanacaste Province was annexed from Nicaragua in one such dispute. In 1838, Costa Rica formally withdrew from the Federation and proclaimed itself sovereign.

32.

    a. Finding little gold or other valuable minerals in Costa Rica, however, the Spanish turned to agriculture.
    b. Because of not finding gold or other valuable minerals in Costa Rica, then, the Spanish turned to agriculture.
    c. There turned out to be no gold or other valuable minerals in Costa Rica, however, the Spanish turned to agriculture.
    d. Finding out about gold or other valuable minerals in Costa Rica, however, the Spanish turned to agriculture.

33.

    a. A tradition where everyone is equal arose in Costa Rica during the early years of Spanish colonization.
    b. A democratic tradition arose in Costa Rica during the early years of Spanish colonization.
    c. An egalitarian tradition arose in Costa Rica during the early years of Spanish colonization.
    d. A commensurate tradition rose up in Costa Rica during the early years of Spanish colonization.

34.
a. The newly independent provinces formed a Federation, because border disputes broke out among them.
b. Although the newly independent provinces formed a Federation, border disputes breaking out among them.
c. The newly independent provinces formed a Federation with the border disputes that broke out among them.
d. Although the newly independent provinces formed a Federation, border disputes broke out among them.

35.
a. Costa Rica's northern Guanacaste Province, was annexed from Nicaragua in one such dispute.
b. Costa Rica's northern Guanacaste Province was annexed, from Nicaragua, in one such dispute.
c. Costa Rica's northern Guanacaste Province was annexed in one such dispute from Nicaragua.
d. Costa Rica's northern Guanacaste Province was annexed from Nicaragua in one such dispute.

Passage II
It's easy to patch a bicycle inner tube! **36**. <u>The technology has been round a long time, and is quite reliable</u> if the job is done properly. Here's how:

37. <u>First select a patch slightly larger than the size of the hole.</u>
Next, use sandpaper to **38**.<u>rough the surface of the tube at an area somewhat larger than the patch</u>.
39.<u>Buff the tube so that it don't shine any more</u>. If there is a molding line in the area where the patch is to be applied, sand it down completely or it will leak.
40.<u>Apply a dab of rubber cement then spread a thin coat</u>. Work quickly.
Allow the cement to dry completely.
Peel the foil from the patch and press the patch onto the tube firmly.
Squeeze the patch tightly onto the tube. **41**.<u>Now, re-inflate the tire and you finished!</u>
This procedure should give you a tire that is as good as new.

36.
a. The technology has been round a long time and is quite reliable
b. The technology has been around a long time, and is quite reliable
c. The technology has been around for a long time, and is quite reliable
d. The technology has been around for a long time and is quite reliable

37.
a. First select a patch slightly larger than the size of the hole.
b. First, select a patch slightly larger than the size of the hole.
c. First select a patch, slightly larger than the size of the hole.
d. First select a patch: slightly larger than the size of the hole.

38.
a. roughen the surface of the tube at an area somewhat larger than the patch.
b. rough up the surface of the tube at an area somewhat larger than the patch.
c. roughen a portion of the tube surface with an area somewhat larger than the patch.
d. roughen the surface of the tube with an area somewhat larger than the patch.

39.

    a. Buff the tube so that it don't shine no more.
    b. Buff the tube so that it doesn't shine any more.
    c. Buff the tube so that it doesn't shine no more.
    d. Buff the tube so that it don't shine.

40.

    a. Applying a dab of rubber cement then spread a thin coat.
    b. Apply a dab of rubber cement then spreads a thin coat.
    c. Apply a dab of rubber cement, and then spread a thin coat.
    d. Apply a dab of rubber cement and, then, spread a thin coat.

41.

    a. Now, re-inflate the tire and you're finished!
    b. Now re-inflate the tire and your finished!
    c. Now, re-inflate the tire and your finished!
    d. Now re-inflate the tire and you've finished!

Passage III

42. Norway's economy relies heavy upon oil and gas. Exports of these commodities account for roughly half of all export earnings. **43.** Other exports include metals ships and fish. Norway is one of the world's top 10 fishing nations. **44.** Agriculture is diversified and is a great deal of livestock, though **45.** more than half of the country's food needs are imported.

42.

    a. Norway's economy relies upon heavy oil and gas.
    b. Norway's economy relies heavily upon oil and gas.
    c. Norways economy relies heavy upon oil and gas.
    d. Norways economy relies heavily upon oil and gas.

43.

    a. Other exports include metal ships and fish.
    b. Other exports includes metals ships and fish.
    c. Other exports include metals ships and fishes.
    d. Other exports include metals, ships, and fish.

44.

    a. Agriculture is diversified and there is a great deal of livestock
    b. Agriculture is diversified and with a great deal of livestock
    c. Agriculture is diversified and includes a great deal of livestock
    d. Agriculture is diversified and has a great deal of livestock

45.

    a. more than half of the country's food is imported
    b. more than half of the countries food needs are imported
    c. more than half the country's food needs are imported
    d. more than half of the countries foods are imported

Passage IV

46. Patient's with tennis elbow are having pain outside of the elbow. It is made worse when grasping objects or drawing back the wrist. The most common symptoms of tennis elbow are pain over the outside of the elbow and pain when lifting objects. **47.** The pain is often radiating down the forearm to the hand.

The pain associated with tennis elbow **48.** usually came on gradually but it could also be sudden. Most patients are between the ages of 35 and 65. **49.** The syndrome affects men and women the same, usually occurring in the dominant arm. **50.** Anyone can be affected, but mostly they were either manual laborers or active sports participants.

46.
   a. Patient's with tennis elbow experience pain outside of the elbow.
   b. Patients with tennis elbow have pain outside of the elbow.
   c. Patients with tennis elbow experience pain on the outside of the elbow.
   d. Patients with tennis elbow pain have it on the outside elbow.

47.
   a. The pain often radiates down the forearm to the hand.
   b. The pain often radiated down the forearm to the hand.
   c. The pain is often goes and radiates down the forearm to the hand.
   d. The pain is often radiation down the forearm to the hand.

48.
   a. usually came on gradually but could also be sudden
   b. usually comes on gradually but may also be sudden
   c. usually comes on gradually, but could also be sudden
   d. usually comes on gradually but is also sudden

49.
   a. The syndrome affects men and women too,
   b. The syndrome affects men and women also,
   c. The syndrome affects men and women similarly,
   d. The syndrome affects men and women the same,

50.
   a. Anyone can be affected, but mostly manual laborers or active sports participants.
   b. Anyone can be affected, but mostly it's either manual laborers or active sports participants.
   c. Anyone can be affected, but most patients were either manual laborers or active sports participants.
   d. Anyone can be affected, but most patients are either manual laborers or active sports participants.

Passage V

The traditional form of home mortgage loan is the fixed rate variety. The term "fixed rate" mortgage refers to the fact that **51.** the interest rate ain't going to change over the life of the loan. The major advantage of this type of loan is that **52.** it is predictable, the payments remain the same over the duration of the loan. Compare this to an adjustable rate mortgage (ARM):
53. in these loans the interest rate and therefore the payment change regularly based upon market conditions. **54.** When interest rates are low, an adjustable rate mortgage may seem like an attractive option however when interest rates go up so will your monthly mortgage payment.

51.

    a. the interest rate don't change over the life of the loan.
    b. the interest rate doesn't change over the life of the loan.
    c. the interest rate won't be going to change over the life of the loan.
    d. the interest rate won't be changing over the life of the loan.

52.

    a. it is predictable, the payments remain the same over the duration of the loan.
    b. it is predictable (the payments remain the same over the duration of the loan).
    c. it is predictable: the payments remain the same over the duration of the loan.
    d. it is predictable; the payments remain the same over the duration of the loan.

53.

    a. in these loans the interest rate and so the payment change regularly
    b. in these loans the interest rate and also the payment change regularly
    c. in these loans the interest rate and even the payment change regularly
    d. in these loans the interest rate, and therefore the payment, change regularly

54.

    a. When interest rates are low, an adjustable rate mortgage may seem like an attractive option. However, when interest rates go up so will your monthly mortgage payment.
    b. When interest rates are low, an adjustable rate mortgage may seem like an attractive option, however, when interest rates go up so will your monthly mortgage payment.
    c. When interest rates are low, an adjustable rate mortgage may seem like an attractive option however when they go up so will your monthly mortgage payment.
    d. When interest rates are low, an adjustable rate mortgage may seem like an attractive option, when interest rates go up so will your monthly mortgage payment.

Reading Skills Practice Questions

Read this article on time studies, then answer Questions 1-3.

<u>Time Studies</u>

The basis of scientific management of manufacturing is the time study. Attributed to F.W. Taylor, a nineteenth century industrial engineer, these studies are used to break an operation down into its elementary units, to determine the best methods and time for the performance of each of these units, and their summation into the total time required for the entire job.

The modern time study usually incorporates motion study. The aim of a motion study is to determine the most effective motion to accomplish a desired result; and one of the elements in the determination of its effectiveness is the time it takes to execute it. Time study and motion study, therefore, go hand in hand, but it is not impossible to make an effective and profitable motion study without the use of any timing device. A classic example of modern motion study – and one of the first of its kind -- is an experiment carried out in 1837. A printing foreman named Lefevre was struck with the fact that the traditional lay-out of the printer's case was not the one best adapted to the setting of type, in that usually the compositor had to reach farthest for the most frequently used letters. Lefevre, therefore, redesigned the case with a view to the maximum economy of effort and, after a test of both lay-outs, adopted the revised case for his plant. After some years of struggle with the traditions of the printing fraternity, the new case was abandoned; but the experiment is a good early illustration of the application of motion study.

Gilbreth was one of the earliest engineers to develop methods for the study and representation of motions. He developed several ingenious appliances for this purpose, including the *chronocyclegraph*, a series of photographs of motions taken by attaching small electric lights to the hands of the operators in such a way that the course of the motion was recorded by the light on the negative as a continuous line. The light could be made to flash at intervals to track the direction of the motion. On the basis of these photographs Gilbreth constructed "motion models," wire contrivances reproducing in three dimensions the lines in the photographs. These models were used to help rehabilitate soldiers wounded during the first World War, and also to study the effects of fatigue on motions performed by factory workers.

1. A main element in determining the effectiveness of a motion is
    a. Which hand is to be used
    b. How it leads to the subsequent motion
    c. The time required to perform it
    d. The strength required to perform it

2. In Lefevre's redesign of the printing case, he
    a. had the compositor reach further for the most frequently used letters
    b. used a timer
    c. was joined by the printing fraternity
    d. placed the most frequently used letters closest to the compositor

3. Gilbreth tracked motions using
   a. photographs
   b. a chronometer
   c. wounded soldiers
   d. printing cases

Find the answers to Questions 4-8 by reading the chart.

Table 1. Consumer Price Index for All Urban Consumers (CPI-U): U.S. city average, by expenditure category and commodity and service group

(1982-84=100, unless otherwise noted)

Item and group	Relative importance, December 2008	Unadjusted indexes		Unadjusted percent change to June 2009 from—		Seasonally adjusted percent change from—		
		May 2009	June 2009	June 2008	May 2009	Mar. to Apr.	Apr. to May	May to June
Expenditure category								
All items	100.000	213.856	215.693	-1.4	0.9	0.0	0.1	0.7
All items (1967=100)	-	640.616	646.121	-	-	-	-	-
Food and beverages	15.757	218.076	218.030	2.2	.0	-.2	-.2	.1
Food	14.629	217.826	217.740	2.1	.0	-.2	-.2	.0
Food at home	8.156	215.088	214.824	.8	-.1	-.6	-.5	.0
Cereals and bakery products	1.150	252.714	253.008	3.0	.1	-.7	-.2	.0
Meats, poultry, fish, and eggs	1.898	203.789	204.031	.6	.1	.0	-.9	-.2
Dairy and related products [1]	.910	196.055	194.197	-7.1	-.9	-1.3	-.5	-.9
Fruits and vegetables	1.194	274.006	272.608	-1.9	-.5	.0	-1.0	1.1
Nonalcoholic beverages and beverage materials	.982	162.803	162.571	2.7	-.1	-1.0	-.1	.1
Other food at home	2.022	191.144	191.328	4.1	.1	-.8	-.1	.0
Sugar and sweets	.300	196.403	197.009	6.2	.3	-.5	.0	.2
Fats and oils	.241	200.679	201.127	2.5	.2	-1.4	-.7	.6
Other foods	1.481	205.587	205.654	3.9	.0	-.8	.0	-.2
Other miscellaneous foods [1][2]	.433	122.838	122.224	3.2	-.5	.4	.0	-.5
Food away from home [1]	6.474	223.023	223.163	3.8	.1	.3	.1	.1
Other food away from home [1][2]	.314	155.099	155.841	4.0	.5	.4	.0	.5
Alcoholic beverages	1.127	220.005	220.477	3.1	.2	-.1	.3	.2
Housing	43.421	216.971	218.071	.1	.5	-.1	-.1	.0
Shelter	33.200	249.779	250.243	1.3	.2	.2	.1	.1
Rent of primary residence [3]	5.957	249.069	249.092	2.7	.0	.2	.1	.1
Lodging away from home [2]	2.478	135.680	138.318	-6.9	1.9	.5	.1	.3
Owners' equivalent rent of primary residence [3][4]	24.433	256.875	256.981	1.9	.0	.1	.1	.1
Tenants' and household insurance [1][2]	.333	120.728	121.083	1.7	.3	-.1	.0	.3
Fuels and utilities	5.431	206.358	212.677	-8.1	3.1	-1.7	-1.3	-.8
Household energy	4.460	183.783	190.647	-10.8	3.7	-2.2	-1.8	-1.0
Fuel oil and other fuels	.301	225.164	232.638	-40.3	3.3	-2.1	-3.1	2.0
Gas (piped) and electricity [3]	4.159	189.619	196.754	-7.8	3.8	-2.2	-1.7	-1.2
Water and sewer and trash collection services [2]	.971	159.517	159.831	6.2	.2	.6	.6	.4
Household furnishings and operations	4.790	129.644	129.623	1.6	.0	.0	.0	.0
Household operations [1][2]	.781	149.468	149.995	1.3	.4	-.1	-.9	.4
Apparel	3.691	121.751	118.799	1.5	-2.4	-.2	-.2	.7
Men's and boys' apparel	.923	117.146	112.849	.7	-3.7	-1.7	.4	-.5
Women's and girls' apparel	1.541	109.460	106.455	2.1	-2.7	.2	-.1	1.6
Infants' and toddlers' apparel	.183	114.142	113.915	2.1	-.2	1.3	-1.6	2.2
Footwear	.688	127.519	125.515	1.6	-1.6	.4	.1	.2
Transportation	15.314	175.997	183.735	-13.2	4.4	-.4	.8	4.2
Private transportation	14.189	171.757	179.649	-13.3	4.6	-.3	.9	4.5
New and used motor vehicles [2]	6.931	92.701	93.020	-.6	.3	.4	.5	.4
New vehicles	4.480	135.162	135.719	.9	.4	.4	.5	.7
Used cars and trucks	1.628	122.650	124.323	-8.6	1.4	-.1	1.0	.9
Motor fuel	3.164	193.609	225.021	-35.2	16.2	-2.6	2.7	17.2
Gasoline (all types)	2.964	193.727	225.526	-34.6	16.4	-2.8	3.1	17.3
Motor vehicle parts and equipment [1]	.382	134.347	134.270	5.0	-.1	.1	-.2	-.1
Motor vehicle maintenance and repair [1]	1.188	242.488	242.683	4.1	.1	.2	-.1	.1
Public transportation	1.125	228.878	232.540	-12.1	1.6	-.8	-1.0	-.5

4. Which of the following expense categories decreased in the year prior to June 2009?
   a. Rent of primary residence
   b. Boys' and men's apparel
   c. Transportation
   d. Meats, fish, and eggs

- 47 -

5. On a seasonally adjusted basis, which of the following decreased by the greatest percentage between April and May of 2009?
    a. Gasoline
    b. Fuel oil and other fuels
    c. Infants' and toddlers' apparel
    d. Fruits and vegetables

6. In the month prior to June 2009, which of the following prices did not change at all?
    a. Public transportation .
    b. Used cars and trucks
    c. Food
    d. Housing

7. According to the organization of the table, which of the following expense categories is not considered to be a component of the "Food at Home" category?
    a. Cereals and bakery products
    b. Fats and oils
    c. Other miscellaneous foods
    d. Alcoholic beverages

8. Which expenditure category was the most important in December of 2008?
    a. Housing
    b. Food and Beverages
    c. Apparel
    d. Transportation

Read this article on food storage, then answer Questions 9-14.

Food Storage Containers

Plastic is one of the most common materials used for food storage. Plastic containers, bags and boxes, are inexpensive, lightweight, and convenient. But is plastic safe? The answer to this question may not be a simple one, as there are many different varieties of plastic, manufactured by different processes. Some of these processes employ phthalates, a type of chemical used to soften the plastic so that it may be molded. And, there is mounting evidence that phthalates may be toxic.

The most common phthalate is *bis*-phenol A, commonly known as BPA. BPA has been declared safe for food storage by the Food and Drug Administration, but the FDA relied on information supplied by the chemical industry to reach that conclusion. Recent evidence has called its decision into doubt, and the agency has announced that it will review its earlier determination.

The concern about BPA's toxicity is widespread, especially when food is stored for young children. Its use in baby bottles has been banned in Canada and in several states in the U.S., and Connecticut has prohibited it in all reusable food containers.

Traces of BPA can be found in foods that have been stored in containers made of polycarbonate and other plastic materials. But these are not limited to baby bottles or to reusable plastic food-storage containers. Canned foods are also found to be contaminated, since plastic linings are often used in food cans to protect the product from taking on the flavor of the metal. The use of plastics in the food industry is widespread, and calls for its elimination have led to predictable protests.

A particular concern is the use of plastic storage containers to microwave food that is to be warmed before serving. BPA has been found to leach from polycarbonates and form other plastics during this process. Caroline Baier-Anderson, a health scientist and an assistant professor in the Department of Epidemiology and Preventive Medicine at the University of Maryland, Baltimore, told the Washington Post: "It is best not to microwave plastics, particularly since alternatives are widely available."

So how can you avoid the potential problems with plastic food storage? You have three major options when it comes to selecting our food storage containers.

1. Use glass containers. Many of these are available with either glass or plastic lids. Some of the plastic lids are BPA-free, but since the lid comes into only limited contact with the product, the presence of BPA is a lesser concern here.

2. Use stainless steel containers. While glass and steel are expensive, they can be used over many times, so that the cost is eventually amortized. They are heavier than plastic, however.

3. Use safer plastic containers. Some manufacturers have responded to consumer concerns by marketing plastics that are BPA-free. There have been some misleading claims however, so that consumers are advised to seek third-party reviews of particular products. One source of information is thegreenguide.com, a website presented by the National Geographic. It has reviews of specific brands of plastic storage products that have been tested for the presence of BPA.

9. What is the main purpose of this article?
   a. To describe the use of plastic in storing food.
   b. To warn readers about a potential danger in using plastic containers for food storage.
   c. To list a variety of different containers that can be used to store food.
   d. To tell readers not to microwave food in plastic containers.

10. Which of the following statements is true, according to the text?
   a. Canada has banned the use of plastics in baby bottles.
   b. Canada has banned the use of plastics in reusable food containers.
   c. Canada has banned the use of BPA in plastics.
   d. Canada has banned the use of BPA in reusable baby bottles.

11. Which of the following statements best reflects the author's point of view in writing this article?
   a. The author feels that all BPA-containing plastics should be banned.
   b. The author feels that BPA-containing plastics should be banned from use in food containers.
   c. The author wants to offer consumers alternatives to using BPA-containing food storage containers.
   d. The author feels that stainless steel food storage containers are the best for all uses.

12. Phthalates are used in manufacturing plastics
   a. to facilitate molding
   b. to make them toxic
   c. to allow them to be microwaved
   d. to make them safer

13. To avoid potential problems with food storage containers, the author suggests
    a. avoiding all plastics
    b. carefully selecting materials
    c. never using plastics in microwave ovens
    d. avoiding plastic baby bottles

14. Which of the following would the author most likely recommend?
    a. Discarding plastic food storage containers after a single use.
    b. Avoiding canned foods.
    c. Moving to Canada or Connecticut if you have a new baby.
    d. Writing to your congressperson for more information about BPA

Read this article on leatherback turtles, then answer Questions 15-19.

Leatherback Turtle Populations Recover

The Pacific leatherback turtle arrives in California during the late summer to feed on offshore jellyfish populations. In recent years, egg poaching and accidental capture of adults by fishing nets have led to severe reductions of leatherback populations throughout the Pacific. Conservation of remaining populations of this endangered species became a priority for the U.S. Fish and Wildlife Service.

Since leatherbacks nest on tropical beaches, it was long thought that the California visitors originated from nearby colonies in Mexico and Central America. But research during the past decade has shown that these populations actually come from nesting colonies in the western Pacific.

The western populations were also shown to be comprised of several groups with distinct feeding and migratory patterns. Although they are genetically identical, some groups feed on California beaches, while others visit beaches in the eastern and southern Pacific. These results have caused the Fish and Wildlife service to alter its approach to conserving the species.

"To help protect the leatherbacks, we have expanded our central California work to include a variety of conservation and research initiatives in western Pacific island nations," said Jeff Seminoff, head of the Southwest Fisheries Center Marine Turtle Ecology and Assessment Team. "We recently conducted aerial surveys in Papua New Guinea, Papua (Indonesia) and the Solomon Islands, confirming that large numbers of nesting leatherbacks remain only on a few beaches in Papua. This underscores the need to protect these last remaining rookeries before it is too late."

A program of sustained beach conservation efforts is now in progress in Papua and throughout the western Pacific. This project coordinates contributions from local organizations, government and university biologists, World Wildlife Fund researchers and fishery management organizations. Local residents are being trained to monitor the nesting beaches and to evaluate hatching success. Early results have inspired a cautious optimism: leatherback turtle populations seem to be recovering.

An important part of local folklore, the leatherback is known by many names throughout the western Pacific: trousel, tabob, penyubelimbing, leddebak. Once an important food source, it figures in the legends of many island peoples. With the new awareness that the turtles travel broadly across the ocean, the new partnership is now working within the international community to ensure survival of the leatherback for future generations.

Continued success of these conservation efforts will require a more complete understanding of the entire ecosystem in which the turtles live. These highly mobile marine reptiles move freely across one third of the globe, roaming the entire Pacific Ocean. An effective program necessitates a broad approach that includes the restoration of feeding grounds, nesting beaches, and the migratory routes that connect them.

As leatherback turtles journey from one edge of the Pacific to the other, these gentle marine ambassadors are bringing governments, communities and people together to share a common cause of preserving vibrant marine ecosystems for future generations.

15. The passage is primarily concerned with
    a. beach conservation efforts in the western Pacific
    b. the occurrence of leatherback turtles in the legends of island peoples
    c. the geographic origins of California leatherback populations
    d. international efforts to protect leatherback habitats

16. The author's tone in this passage is best described as
    a. hectoring
    b. factual
    c. mobilizing
    d. dismissive

17. California's leatherbacks were thought to come from beaches in Mexico because
    a. these beaches are relatively close
    b. they prefer warm water
    c. they are poor swimmers
    d. they are genetic variants

18. The article tells us that leatherback turtle populations are presently
    a. recovering rapidly due to conservation efforts
    b. an important source of food for many native populations
    c. highly mobile
    d. recovering on a small scale

19. The article implies that effective measures to protect the leatherback turtle will require an understanding of
    a. native myths
    b. the diet of Third World people
    c. a combination of interacting factors
    d. foreign governments

Read this passage about teaching children about money, then answer Questions 20-24.

Have you ever bought your child a toy to calm a tantrum? Most parents experience moments like this, moments where money comes into play. But money doesn't always buy happiness, especially when it comes to kids.

Kids start learning about money from a very early age. In fact, today's children have more money than ever: extra income spent on snacks, toys, and clothing. It is estimated that more than 10 million youths between the ages of 10 and 18 receive regular allowances from their parents, averaging over $50 per week.

While today's young people may have more money to spend than ever before, their understanding of savings and values hasn't improved. For example, most young people don't know how to calculate the interest earned on a savings account. For the most part, they don't understand how to manage debt or invest for future expenses like college tuition.

Educators say that parents should teach their children about financial responsibility. Early lessons will go a long way toward fostering positive attitudes and habits later in life. Young children learn about money through everyday activities like grocery shopping, and watching their parents pay bills and withdraw cash from the ATM. Family discussions can also help. Take the time to explain the basics to your child: that there is a certain amount of money that comes into the household and a certain amount of money that goes out, and that essential expenses-food, utilities, and clothing- must be paid from that money.

Most children have no idea where money comes from. Ask them, and they will say, "From the ATM machine." Take the time to explain to your children that you must work to earn your money, that you must put it into the bank before you can withdraw it from the ATM machine. Giving a child an allowance tied to the performance of certain family chores is an excellent way to teach this concept.

Here are some ideas for interacting with your children on the subject of money:

Talk money. Routinely discuss how money is earned and spent. Explain your purchasing decisions: "We are buying apples because they are on sale" or "We need electricity so I have to pay the bill."

Model behavior. Children develop their attitudes from what they see you do, not what they hear you say. A lesson on the value of money might also involve family activities: "Let's rent a movie instead of all going to the theater. We can save for our family vacation."

Set limits. Even if you can buy everything your child asks for, consider the wisdom of setting some boundaries. Learn to say no to your child and be firm.

Provide freedom. As your children grow up and learn more, let them make their own decisions about money and personal finances. Support their decision-making with advice, but gradually cede the final decision.
Teach saving. For young children, a personal piggy bank is a good way to introduce concepts of money and savings. Early opportunities to save help develop a lifelong respect for the value of money. Money can be set aside for a favorite toy, as well as for future goals like college or a car.

20. This passage is best described as
    a. humorous
    b. factual
    c. advising
    d. dramatic

21. The purpose of the first paragraph is to
    a. capture attention by relating the topic to something in the reader's personal experience.
    b. introduce the topic of tantrums.
    c. suggest that rich children are not happy.
    d. show how money can be used to induce children to behave well.

22. The article argues that
    a. young children should not be trusted with money.
    b. parents should discuss money with children from an early age.
    c. children should be given ATM cards.
    d. parents should buy children whatever they can afford.

23. One suggestion in the article about allowances is that they
    a. should be generous.
    b. should not be given.
    c. should be tied to some responsibilities.
    d. should be given on a monthly basis.

24. The author is of the opinion that
    a. children should be given no say in money matters.
    b. children should be allowed to spend their own money however they wish.
    c. children should not be given money at all.
    d. children should be given increasing freedom to make their own decisions about how to spend money.

Read the following paragraph, then answer Questions 25-28.

The Nigerian Letter Fraud

Nigerian letter frauds are variations of advance fee schemes in which a letter, mailed from Nigeria, offers the recipient the "opportunity" to share in millions of dollars that the author, a self-proclaimed government official, is trying to transfer illegally out of Nigeria. The victim receives a letter or email asking him to send personal information: blank letterhead stationery, bank name and account numbers and other identifying information. Eventually, the scheme attempts to get the willing victim, who has demonstrated a propensity for larceny by responding to the invitation, to send money to the author of the letter in Nigeria in several installments of increasing amounts for a variety of reasons. Payment of taxes, bribes to government officials, and legal fees are often described in great detail with the promise that all expenses will be reimbursed as soon as the funds are spirited out of Nigeria. In reality, the millions of dollars do not exist and the victim gets nothing. In fact, once the victim stops sending money, the perpetrators have been known to use the personal information that they received to impersonate the victim, draining bank accounts and credit card balances. While such an invitation strikes most of us as a laughable hoax, millions of dollars in losses are caused by these schemes annually.

25. This paragraph is best described as
    a. factual reporting
    b. humor
    c. fiction
    d. poetry

26. A "propensity for larceny" is
   a. a desire for compensation
   b. a proclivity for theft
   c. a talent for robbery
   d. a disinclination for pilferage

27. The hoax described in the paragraph attempts to get the victim to send money to the perpetrator in order to
   a. show good faith
   b. pay Nigerian taxes
   c. buy stationery
   d. help the perpetrator escape persecution

28. According to the text, the Nigerian letter gambit is
   a. a laughable attempt to defraud people that has little chance of success
   b. a good reason not to open email attachments
   c. sometimes legitimate
   d. surprisingly successful

Read the following passage, then answer Questions 29-32.

(Adapted from "Roughing It", by Mark Twain).

After fifteen days of hiking along the Humboldt River, we reached Unionville. People who are used to the Mississippi grow accustomed to associating the term "river" with a great deal of watery grandeur. Consequently, such a person may feel rather disappointed to find that he can jump across the Humboldt until he is overheated, then drink it dry.

Unionville consists of eleven cabins built in a deep crevice on a bleak mountainside. The mountain walls rise so steeply around it that the sun only touches the rooftops for an hour out of each day. We built a small, rude cabin in the side of the crevice and roofed it with canvas, leaving a corner open to serve as a chimney, through which the cattle used to tumble occasionally, at night, and mash our furniture and interrupt our sleep. It was very cold weather and fuel for the fire was scarce. We shivered and bore it.

I confess that I had expected to see the mountains glittering with gold. I expected it to litter the ground, waiting to be picked up. Some suspicion that this might be an exaggerated notion kept me from sharing my expectation with my friends, yet I was perfectly satisfied in my own mind that, within a few days at the most, I would gather up gold enough to make me satisfactorily wealthy. And so, at the first opportunity, I sauntered nonchalantly away from the cabin, keeping an eye on the boys and stopping to contemplate the sky when they seemed to look at me.. then, as soon as the coast was clear, I fled away as guiltily as a thief might have done and never halted till I was far beyond sight and call. Then, I began my feverish search for the riches of the mountains.

By and by, in the bed of a shallow rivulet, I found a deposit of shining yellow scales, and my breath almost forsook me. A gold mine! Picking up a bright fragment, I hid behind a boulder and polished it and scrutinized it with a nervous eagerness. It shone brightly in the light of the sun. I set about scooping out more, and for an hour I toiled down the windings of the stream and robbed its bed. But at last the descending sun warned me to give up the quest, and I turned homeward laden with wealth.

The boys were as hungry as usual, but I could eat nothing. Neither could I talk. I was full of dreams and far away. Their conversation kept interrupting my thoughts, annoying me at first, but presently I became amused. Here they were, talking of privations and small economies that must be made, when our very own gold mine lay but a mile away. I decided to break the news to them calmly and to watch the play of emotions on their faces. I said:

"Where have you all been?"

"Prospecting."

"What did you find?"

"Nothing."

"Nothing? What do you think of the country?"

"Can't tell, yet," said Mr. Ballou, who was an experienced gold-miner. "It's fair enough here, maybe, but overrated. We won't starve, but we aren't going to get rich, here, either."

"So you think the prospects are pretty poor, eh?"

"I guess that's so, but we'll try it for a bit."

"Suppose, now," I put forth, "suppose you could find a ledge that would yield, say, a hundred and fifty dollars a ton—would that satisfy you?"

"Try us once!" from the whole party.

"Or suppose—merely a supposition, of course— suppose you were to find a ledge that would yield two thousand dollars a ton—would that satisfy you?"

"Here—what do you mean? What are you coming at? Is there some mystery behind all this?"

"Gentlemen," said I, "I am but a mere novice, of course, and don't know anything—but all I ask of you is to cast your eye on this and tell me what you think of it!" and I tossed my treasure before them.

There was an eager scrabble for it, and a closing of heads together over it under the candle-light. Then old Ballou said:

"Think of it? I think it is nothing but a lot of granite rubbish and nasty glittering mica that isn't worth ten cents an acre!"

So vanished my dream. So melted my wealth away. So toppled my airy castle to the earth and left me stricken and forlorn.

Moralizing, I observed, then, that "all that glitters is not gold."

So I learned then that gold in its native state is but dull, un-ornamental stuff, and that only low-born metals excite the admiration of the ignorant with an ostentatious glitter. However, like the rest of the world, I still go on underrating men of gold and glorifying men of mica.

29. Which of the following best describes the nature and tone of the passage?
    a. adventure
    b. history
    c. drama
    d. caricature

30. In the second paragraph, the author describes cattle falling through the chimney of the cabin from the steep hillside above. This is an example of
    a. burlesque
    b. illustrative detail
    c. character development
    d. denouement

31. Mr. Ballou is able to recognize that the author's find has no value because
    a. he is a mineralogist
    b. he has mined gold before
    c. he compares it to a gold watch
    d. he bites down on it to see if it is hard

32. The author concludes the passage with
    a. a lament about lost riches
    b. a comparison of minerals and men
    c. an angry denunciation of mica
    d. the hope that he will find gold the next day

Read the work instruction below, then answer questions 33-37.

JOB HAZARDS ANALYSIS

1.0 PURPOSE AND SCOPE

This procedure describes the Job Hazard Analysis (JHA) process for identifying, evaluating, controlling, and communicating potential hazards and environmental impacts associated with operations or work by the Tank Operations Contractor (TOC). It applies to all TOC work activities, including the performance of field work involving general plant maintenance, operations, and environmental remediation. This procedure applies to subcontractors who do not have an approved job hazard analysis process.

Everyone is required to work safely and to maintain a safe work environment. Training procedures have been reviewed to ensure that workers are trained to the general hazards associated with work at the tank farms. Visitors should be briefed on the general safety hazards they may be exposed to and controls expected of them as part of their orientation.

2.0 IMPLEMENTATION
This procedure is effective on the date shown in the header.

3.0 RESPONSIBILITIES
Responsibilities are contained within Section 4.0.

4.0 Methods for Implementation of Controls
In order to effectively implement necessary controls to mitigate or eliminate hazards to the workers, the following guidelines should be used:

4.1. The following hierarchy of methods to eliminate or mitigate hazards shall be used in descending order, when feasible and appropriate:
A. Eliminate the hazard or substitution (e.g., different chemical cleaning agent)
B. Utilize engineering controls (e.g., ventilation)
C. Administrative controls (e.g., dose monitoring)
D. Personal protective equipment (PPE) (e.g., self-contained breathing apparatus)

4.2. Controls within the qualification or training of the worker that are often used do not need to be discussed in the work instructions. Examples: Use of leather gloves, safety glasses of the proper type that the worker normally uses.

4.3. Controls within the qualification or training of the worker that are seldom used, and are applicable to the entire work activity, should be placed in the precautions as a reminder that the hazard exists and the workers are expected to take the appropriate actions. Examples: Use of hearing protection due to a noisy environment at the job site, or observation of overhead lines when they are present at the job site.

4.4. Controls within the qualification and training of the workers, but for hazards that are introduced at specific steps or by specific actions during the job, should have a warning or caution statement immediately prior to the step but require no detailed mitigation instructions in the work instructions. Example: a warning for the release of pressure when breaching a system that may have residual pressure.

4.5. Controls not within the qualification and training of the workers for hazards should have detailed instructions for how the workers are to mitigate the hazard and should be in the work instructions or procedure in a way that is prominent and prevents or mitigates the hazard. Example: the steps required to successfully release the pressure on a system in an operation which is not normally performed.

33. This document is
    a. a government request for proposals
    b. a process for making rules for working safely
    c. a portion of a contract
    d. a set of rules for working efficiently

34. According to the procedure, if a worker is exposed to a hazardous chemical, which of the following is the last thing that should be tried to prevent injury or illness?
    a. Use a different chemical.
    b. Install fans to keep fumes away from the worker.
    c. Measure the amount of exposure of each affected worker.
    d. Give the worker protective clothing.

- 57 -

35. Welders must always use goggles and are taught to use them as part of their basic training. According to the text, the use of goggles during specific welding operations should
    a. be prominently displayed at the beginning of the work instruction.
    b. be displayed as a caution prior to the welding step described in the work instruction.
    c. be described in detail in the work instruction.
    d. not be discussed in the work instruction.

36. This passage would normally need to be read and understood by
    a. managers at the site.
    b. laborers at the site.
    c. visitors to the site.
    d. workers making deliveries to the site.

37. Which of the following requires the most comprehensive description within the work instructions?
    a. Controls that are part of the worker's training and are used routinely
    b. Controls that are part of the worker's training but that are seldom used
    c. Controls that are part of the worker's training and that are required for specific steps in the work procedure
    d. Controls that are not part of the worker's training

Read the following dialogue, then answer Questions 38-42.

Adapted from Moliere: "Le Medecin Malgre Lui"

DOCTOR

The Doctor and his wife come onstage quarreling.

Doctor: No, I tell you, I will do nothing of the kind. After all, I am the master.

Martine: And I tell you that I didn't go and marry you to put up with all your freaks.

Doctor: Oh, what an awful trouble it is to have a wife! How right Aristotle was when he said that a woman is worse than the devil!

Martine: Just listen to the clever man, with his fool of an Aristotle.

Doctor: Clever, indeed! You go and find a ditch-digger who can reason like me about everything, who has served for six years a most famous doctor, and who in his youth could say the Latin grammar by heart.

Martine: Plague take the fool!

Doctor: Plague take the wench!

Martine: Cursed be the day when I took it into my head to go and say "Yes!"

Doctor: Cursed be the old idiot who made me sign my ruin!

Martine: It becomes you well to complain of our marriage! You should thank Heaven every moment of your life for having me as a wife. And did you deserve, tell me, to marry a woman like me?

Doctor: True, indeed! You honored me too much, and I had reason to be satisfied on our wedding-day. Gad! Don't make me speak of it, or I might say certain things.
Martine: Well! What is it you'd say?

Doctor: Enough of that. It is sufficient that I know what I know, and that you were very lucky to have me.

Martine: What do you mean by my being lucky to have you? A man who reduces me to beggary; a debauched, deceitful villain, who eats up all I possess.

Doctor: That's a lie; I drink part of it.

Martine: Who sells, bit by bit, all that we have in the house.

Doctor: That is what is called living on one's means.

Martine: Who even sold the bed from under me.

Doctor: You'll get up all the earlier.

Martine: A man who does not leave a single stick of furniture in the house.

Doctor: We move about more easily.

Martine: And who does nothing from morning to night but drink and gamble.

Doctor: That's for fear of depression.

Martine: And what can I do with the children all the time?

Doctor: Anything you like.

Martine: I have four little ones on my hands.

Doctor: Put them down on the ground.

Martine: They do nothing but ask for bread.

Doctor: Whip them. When I have eaten and drunk my fill, I wish everybody to live on the fat of the land.

Martine (threatening, moves toward him): And do you think, drunkard, that things can always go on like this?

Doctor: Now, my wife, gently, if you please.

Martine: That I must endure for ever your insolence and excesses.

Doctor (backing away): Do not get in a passion, my dear wife.

Martine: And that I shall not find the means of bringing you to a sense of your duty?
Doctor (standing his ground): My dear wife, you know that I am not very patient, and that I have a good strong arm.

38. This play is an example of a
    a. tragedy
    b. comedy
    c. drama
    d. soliloquy

39. When the Doctor curses "the old idiot who made me sign my ruin", he is referring to
    a. someone who loaned him money
    b. someone who sold him his house
    c. the clergyman who married him to Martine
    d. a government official

40. When Martine criticizes the Doctor's bad habits, such as drinking and gambling, his answers may be described as
    a. glib
    b. regretful
    c. defensive
    d. apologetic

41. Which of the following best describes the Doctor's personality?
    a. irascible
    b. intolerant
    c. irresponsible
    d. choleric

42. When Martine grows angry and moves toward him, threateningly, what is the Doctor's first response?
    a. He grows angry as well.
    b. He shows fear.
    c. He ignores her.
    d. He attempts to placate her.

Read the following instructions, then answer Questions 43-44.

Application Instructions: American Institute for the Written Arts, Grants and Awards Program (excerpt)

WORK SAMPLES
Manuscripts must be submitted by applicants in Screenwriting, Playwriting, and Literature (poetry, fiction, and creative nonfiction).

Manuscripts should include a title page with your name, address, and year the work was completed. All pages must be numbered. All writing samples, including previously published work, must be submitted in 12-point.

Photocopied excerpts from books or periodicals in published form are not accepted. Instead, publication, performance, or production information must be restricted to the résumé.

Fiction and creative nonfiction writers must submit 10-20 pages from several short works, or a portion from no more than two larger works, and they must be labeled fiction or nonfiction. If your work is an excerpt, include a one-page statement in the manuscript about where it fits into the whole to orient the reviewers. Poets must submit 10-15 pages of poetry. Shorter poems should be printed one to a page.

Fellowship and Writer-in-Residence applicants must submit one copy of work with applicant name throughout and one copy without applicant name. There should be no identifying marks on the anonymous copy.

Writer-in-Residence applicants must also include one standard size audiotape or CD with up to ten minutes of the applicant reading aloud from his or her own work. The case must be labeled with applicant's name, title of work, and date written. Do not use your name on the audio portion of your reading. (Work samples will not be returned.)

Screenwriters and playwrights must submit 10 to 20 pages from one or two works. Applicants are encouraged to include a one-page synopsis. If screenwriters and playwrights are submitting produced works, they must submit a videotape work sample.

43. Information describing publication or other production of the work samples must be
    a. included with the sample.
    b. prominently displayed.
    c. kept separate from the sample.
    d. submitted as an audio tape.

44. Excerpts must be accompanied by
    a. an anonymous copy.
    b. a videotape work sample.
    c. a label indicating whether the work is fiction or nonfiction.
    d. a statement indicating where the text fits into the larger work.

Mathematics Computation Practice Questions

1. 4.73 – 2.13 =
    a. 6.96
    b. 2.60
    c. 2.50
    d. 2.63
    e. None of these

2. Solve the equation for x: $x + 7 = 11$
    a. $x = 3$
    b. $x = 4$
    c. $x = -4$
    d. $x = -3$
    e. None of these

3. 1.02 + 0.0003 =
    a. 1.0007
    b. 1.023
    c. 1.0203
    d. 1.23
    e. None of these

4. $68 \times \dfrac{1}{4} =$
    a. $\dfrac{69}{4}$
    b. 272
    c. $\dfrac{4}{69}$
    d. 17
    e. None of these

5. 20% of 19 =
    a. 1.9
    b. 2.9
    c. 3.8
    d. 9.5
    e. None of these

6. $\dfrac{18}{4} \div 0.3 =$

    a. 1.5

    b. 15

    c. $\dfrac{15}{4}$

    d. $\dfrac{1.8}{12}$

    e. None of these

7. $\dfrac{8}{7} \div \dfrac{12}{7} =$

    a. 1

    b. $\dfrac{3}{2}$

    c. 0.5

    d. $\dfrac{3}{4}$

    e. None of these

8. $4 - (3 - 1)^2 =$

    a. 0

    b. 1

    c. 2

    e. 3

    e. None of these

9. $\dfrac{-27}{-3} =$

    a. 30

    b. – 30

    c. 9

    d. – 9

    e. None of these

10. $\sqrt{36} =$

    a. 3

    b. 6

    c. 9

    d. 12

    e. None of these

11. 5 x 0 =
   a. 5
   b. 50
   c. 0
   d. 0.5
   e. None of these

12. $6\dfrac{5}{8} + 3\dfrac{7}{8} =$
   a. $9\dfrac{5}{8}$
   b. $11\dfrac{1}{8}$
   c. $10\dfrac{5}{8}$
   d. $10\dfrac{1}{2}$
   e. None of these

13. 16 + (- 4) -7 =
   a. 13
   b. 27
   c. 11
   d. 5
   e. None of these

14. 4.302 + 6.71 =
   a. 11.12
   b. 11.012
   c. 12.11
   d. 10.1012
   e. None of these

15. 7.19 – (-3.2) =
   a. 10.39
   b. 3.99
   c. 9.99
   d. 9.39
   e. None of these

16. $8.65 + \dfrac{1}{4} =$
   a. 10.9
   b. 8.6525
   c. 8.9
   d. 8.654
   e. None of these

17. 36 is ___% of 60.
   a. 40%
   b. 50%
   c. 55%
   d. 60%
   e. None of these

18. Solve for k if $\frac{1}{2}k + 6 = 9$
   a. k = 12
   b. k = 3
   c. k = 6
   d. k = 9
   e. None of these

19. $\frac{3^7}{3^5} =$
   a. 3
   b. 6
   c. 9
   d. 27
   e. None of these

20. $7 - (-4) - 4 =$
   a. – 1
   b. 1
   c. 15
   d. 11
   e. None of these

21. $6\frac{3}{13} + 2\frac{4}{13} =$
   a. $8\frac{7}{26}$
   b. $8\frac{7}{13}$
   c. $7\frac{8}{13}$
   d. $8\frac{1}{13}$
   e. None of these

- 65 -

22. 30% of 1000 =
    a. 30
    b. 60
    c. 300
    d. 3
    e. None of these

23. $\dfrac{8}{18} \div \dfrac{4}{18} =$
    a. 2
    b. 4
    c. $\dfrac{2}{18}$
    d. $\dfrac{6}{18}$
    e. None of these

24. $81.09 \div 0.9 =$
    a. 9.01
    b. 9.1
    c. 90.01
    d. 90.1
    e. None of these

25. $4^2 + 4 =$
    a. 43
    b. 12
    c. 16
    d. 20
    e. None of these

26. $\dfrac{7}{3} \times \dfrac{2}{3} =$
    a. $\dfrac{14}{9}$
    b. $\dfrac{14}{3}$
    c. $\dfrac{9}{3}$
    d. $\dfrac{9}{6}$
    e. None of these

27. $(6 - 4) \times 2 =$
    a. – 2
    b. 2
    c. 4
    d. – 4
    e. None of these

28. $6^2 + 6^0 =$
    a. 6
    b. 36
    c. 7
    d. 37
    e. None of these

29. $23.01 - 2.999 =$
    a. 20.11
    b. 20.011
    c. 21.01
    d. 21.001
    e. None of these

30. $(5 \times 20) \div 4 =$
    a. 20
    b. 22
    c. 25
    d. 33
    e. None of these

31. $- 15 - (6 \times 3) =$
    a. 3
    b. 33
    c. – 33
    d. – 3
    e. None of these

32. Solve for x if $32 = x^2 - 4$
    a. $x = 6$
    b. $x = 36$
    c. $x = 4$
    d. $x = 8$
    e. None of these

33. $6\frac{1}{3} - 4\frac{2}{9} =$

    a. $2\frac{2}{9}$

    b. $2\frac{1}{9}$

    c. $2\frac{2}{6}$

    d. $-2\frac{1}{6}$

    e. None of these

34. 30% of _____ = 18
    a. 54
    b. 60
    c. 66
    d. 75
    e. None of these

35. $\sqrt{81} - \sqrt{25} =$
    a. $\sqrt{56}$
    b. 56
    c. 2
    d. 4
    e. None of these

36. 6 – 7 x 2 - 1 =
    a. - 9
    b. - 3
    c. - 15
    d. - 14
    e. None of these

37. $9 \div (9 - 6)^2 =$

    a. $\frac{1}{5}$

    b. $\frac{9}{5}$

    c. 1
    d. 3
    e. None of these

38. – 12 (– 4 + 3) =
    a. 144
    b. -144
    c. 12
    d. – 12
    e. None of these

39. $\dfrac{85}{18} \div \dfrac{17}{18} =$
    a. $\dfrac{1}{5}$
    b. 5
    c. $\dfrac{34}{9}$
    d. $\dfrac{51}{9}$
    e. None of these

40. 23% of 10,000 =
    a. 23
    b. 230
    c. 2300
    d. 460
    e. None of these

Applied Mathematics Practice Questions

1. Bob buys the newspaper every day for $1.50. If he subscribes, he pays only $3.50 per week for seven issues. How much will his weekly savings be if he subscribes?
   a. $2.00
   b. $4.50
   c. $5.00
   d. $7.00

2. Thirty-five boys went out for the soccer team. Of these, $\frac{5}{7}$ made the team. Of the boys who made the team, $\frac{4}{5}$ showed up for practice on Wednesday. How many boys were at the Wednesday practice?
   a. 18
   b. 20
   c. 22
   d. 25

3. Jamal hosts a dinner in a restaurant for a number of his customers and the bill comes to $1128.08 The restaurant always adds an 18% tip for large groups, and this is included in the total. How much was the total before the tip was added?
   a. $1010.08
   b. $925.02
   c. $956.00
   d. $988.05

Look at the figure below, which shows a coordinate grid. Then answer Questions 4-6.

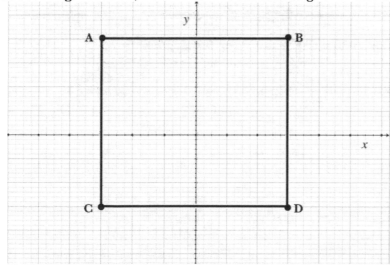

4. Which point has the coordinates (-3,4)?
   a. A
   b. B
   c. C
   d. D

5. What is the distance between points A and C?
   a. 6 units
   b. 7 units
   c. 8 units
   d. 9 units

6. What is the perimeter of the rectangle $ABCD$?
   a. 13 units
   b. 20 units
   c. 26 units
   d. 30 units

7. Evaluate $x^2 - (2y - 3)$ if $x = 4$ and $y = 3$.
   a. 12
   b. 13
   c. 10
   d. 8

8. During a 60 minute television show, the entertainment portion lasted 15 minutes less than 4 times the advertising portion. How long was the entertainment portion?
   a. 30 minutes
   b. 40 minutes
   c. 45 minutes
   d. 50 minutes

9. Which number is missing in the numerical sequence 18, 15, ___, 9, 6 ?
   a. 12
   b. 14
   c. 10
   d. 8

In the figure below, lines $L1$ and $L2$ are parallel to each other. Look at the figure and answer Questions 10 – 13.

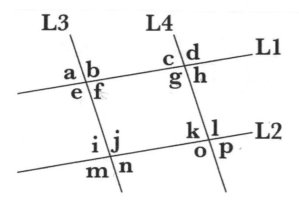

10. If angle $\angle a$ has a measure of 70°, what is the measure of angle $\angle b$?
    a. 30°
    b. 90°
    c. 100°
    d. 110°

11. If angle $\angle a$ has a measure of 70°, what is the measure of angle $\angle i$?
    a. 30°
    b. 60°
    c. 70°
    d. 110°

12. If angle $\angle n$ is congruent to angle $\angle p$, which of the following statements must be true?
    a. Line L3 is perpendicular to line L4
    b. Line L3 is parallel to line L4
    c. Line L3 must eventually intersect line L4
    d. Line $L3$ is parallel to line $L1$

13. If line $L3$ is parallel to line $L4$, which of the following statements must be true?
    a. Angle $\angle f$ is congruent to angle $\angle k$, and angle $\angle a$ is congruent to angle $\angle p$.
    b. Angle $\angle f$ is congruent to angle $\angle k$, and angle $\angle g$ is congruent to angle $\angle p$.
    c. Angle $\angle f$ is congruent to angle $\angle k$, and angle $\angle g$ is congruent to angle $\angle h$.
    d. Angle $\angle f$ is congruent to angle $\angle k$, and angle $\angle g$ is congruent to angle $\angle n$.

14. A jar contains 200 marbles. Thirty of them are blue, 80 are red, and the remainder are yellow. If Natasha reaches blindly into the jar and withdraws a marble at random, what is the probability that it will be blue?
    a. 30%
    b. 20%
    c. 15%
    d. 12%

Look at the following table, which shows the results of a qualification exam given to applicants for public service jobs in Montgomery County. Then, answer Questions 15 – 17.

Score	Under 65	65 – 74	75 – 85	85 – 94	95 - 100	Totals
Men	3	16	24	12	0	55
Women	3	18	20	20	2	63
Totals	6	34	44	32	2	118

15. Approximately what percentage of men passed the exam if 75 is considered to be the cutoff passing grade?
    a. 55%
    b. 65%
    c. 75%
    d. 85%

16. Approximately what percentage of applicants received a grade of 85 or higher?
    a. 25%
    b. 34%
    c. 29%
    d. 32%

17. Based on the table, how many women received a grade that was higher than that of the highest-scoring man?
    a. 0
    b. At least 2
    c. At least 4
    d. 22

18. Morgan plans to replace the floor in his bedroom with square tiles that have a side of 12 inches. The bedroom is 15 feet wide and 18 feet long, and Morgan can lay 9 tiles per hour. How long will the job take?
    a. 30 hours
    b. 18 hours
    c. 10.5 hours
    d. 12 hours

19. Tamara has 5 pair of socks in her drawer. Each pair is a different color. If she pulls out two socks at random, one at a time, what is the probability that they will be of matching colors?
    a. $\dfrac{1}{5}$
    b. $\dfrac{1}{25}$
    c. $\dfrac{1}{10}$
    d. $\dfrac{1}{9}$

20. The first three members of a 4-man swimming team swim their laps in 22.4 seconds, 23.8 seconds, and 21.9 seconds, respectively. How fast must the fourth man swim his lap for the team to average 22 seconds?
    a. 21.0 seconds
    b. 19.9 seconds
    c. 19.5 seconds
    d. 20.2 seconds

Look at the chart below, which shows average reading scores from five rural public schools in standardized tests administered in 2006 and 2007. Then, answer Questions 21-23.

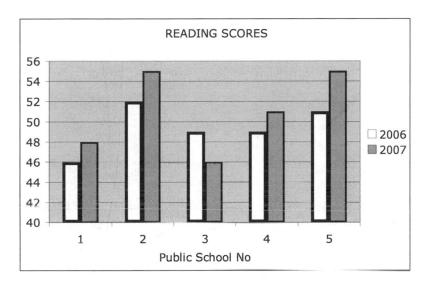

21. Which public school had the lowest average reading score in 2007?
    a. School 1
    b. School 3
    c. School 4
    d. School 5

22. Which public school registered the greatest improvement in reading scores from 2006 to 2007?
    a. School 1
    b. School 2
    c. School 4
    d. School 5

23. What was the highest average reading score obtained by any of the schools during 2006?
    a. 52
    b. 53
    c. 54
    d. 55

24. Sunil uses his cell phone an average of 1200 minutes per month. Which of the following cell phone monthly payment plans will be the least expensive for him?
   a. 10¢ per minute with no base fee
   b. $50 base fee for 600 minutes; 12¢ for each additional minute
   c. $75 base fee for 900 minutes; 14¢ for each additional minute
   d. $100 for 1000 minutes; 18¢ for each additional minute

25. Evaluate the following expression if $u = 3$ and $v = 4$: $\dfrac{1}{3}u^2 + \dfrac{3v}{4} =$
   a. 21
   b. 18
   c. 12
   d. 6

26. Rouenna has to drive 500 miles to Portland. Her car gets 25 miles per gallon and gasoline costs $3 per gallon. What will the trip cost?
   a. $20
   b. $60
   c. $75
   d. $150

Look at the following table, which shows the prices of five company stocks at the close of trading on the stock market one day in April. then, answer Questions 27-28.

Company	Price
IBM	127
Intel	21
Cisco	24
Apple	193
Microsoft	30

27. What is the mean share price of the stocks shown in the table?
   a. 21
   b. 193
   c. 79
   d. 30

28. What is the median share price of the stocks shown in the table?
   a. 21
   b. 193
   c. 79
   d. 30

Look at the chart below, which shows the average amounts that Americans spend on various expense categories. Then, answer Questions 29-30.

Expense Categories

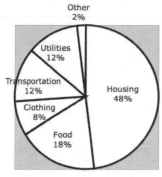

29. Which category represents the greatest expense for the average American?
    a. Food
    b. Housing
    c. Transportation
    d. Clothing

30. If an average American spends a total of $40,000 per year, how much would he or she spend on clothing, according to the chart?
    a. $32,000
    b. $3,200
    c. $320
    d. $2,400

31. Solve the following proportion for x: $\dfrac{-3}{x} = \dfrac{2}{8}$.

    a. x = 3
    b. x = 12
    c. x = -2
    d. x = -12

32. A culture of yeast cells doubles in number every half hour. After 3 hours, there are 6400 yeast cells in the culture. How many were there when the culture was started?
    a. 100
    b. 200
    c. 400
    d. 800

33. Mischa drives from Town A to Town B at 90 kilometers per hour. Brenda drives the same route at 60 kilometers per hour and it takes her 3 hours longer. How far apart are Town A and Town B?
    a. 540 km
    b. 600 km
    c. 480 km
    d. 510 km

Look at the figure below, which shows an isosceles triangle △ABC on top of a rectangle BCED. Then, answer Questions 34-36.

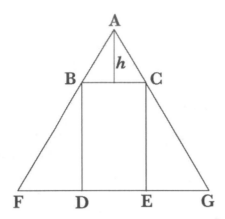

34. Let the area of triangle △ABC be 240 square centimeters, and the height, h, be 20 cm. What is the area of the rectangle BCED if its height is twice the height of △ABC ?
    a. 1144 cm²
    b. 1068 cm²
    c. 960 cm²
    d. 948 cm²

35. See the information given in Question 34. What is the area of the triangle △AFG?
    a. 720 cm²
    b. 2880 cm²
    c. 1860 cm²
    d. 2160 cm²

36. See the information given in Question 34. What is the area of triangle △BFD?
    a. 720 cm²
    b. 480 cm²
    c. 520 cm²
    d. 640 cm²

37. Alfredo works 40 hours per week at an hourly wage of $20. For any overtime, he makes $30 per hour. This week Alfredo made $950. How many hours did he work?
    a. 40
    b. 42
    c. 45
    d. 48

38. What is the next term in the number series 3, 6, 12, 24, ____?
    a. 30
    b. 36
    c. 42
    d. 48

- 77 -

39. The price-earnings (PE) ratio of a stock is the ratio of the share price divided by the annual earnings per share. Company A has issued 3 million shares of stock, which are selling at $6.00 per share. If the PE ratio is 12, how much did Company A earn in the past year?
  a. $1.5 million
  b. $3.0 million
  c. $4.5 million
  d. $6.0 million

Look at the table below, which compares the orbits of the planets in our solar system. Then, answer Questions 40-43.

Property	Mercury	Venus	Earth	Mars	Jupiter	Saturn	Uranus	Neptune
Diameter (km)	4,878	12,104	12,756	6,787	142,800	120,000	51,118	49,528
Mass (Earth=1)	0.055	0.815	1	0.107	318	95	15	17
Average distance from Sun (Earth = 1)	0.39	0.72	1	1.52	5.20	9.54	19.18	30.06
Orbital period (Earth years)	0.24	0.62	1	1.88	11.86	29.46	84.01	164.8
Average orbital speed (km/sec)	47.89	35.03	29.79	24.13	13.06	9.64	6.81	5.43
Gravity (Earth=1)	0.38	0.9	1	0.38	2.64	0.93	0.89	1.12

40. Which of the following statements is true?
  a. The greater a planet's mass, the longer its orbital period.
  b. The larger a planet's diameter, the greater its gravity.
  c. The further a planet is from the Sun, the longer its orbital period.
  d. The greater a planet's mass, the greater its gravity.

41. The mass of the Earth is approximately 6×10^{24} kilograms. What is the mass of Venus?
  a. 4.9×10^{24} kilograms
  b. 4.9×10^{23} kilograms
  c. 0.81×10^{24} kilograms
  d. 8.1×10^{24} kilograms

42. Which of the following statements is true?
  a. The greater a planet's orbital period, the faster its orbital speed.
  b. The closer a planet is to the Sun, the faster its orbital speed.
  c. The smaller a planet's diameter, the faster its orbital speed.
  d. The smaller a planet's mass, the faster its orbital speed.

43. The average distance from the Earth to the Sun is 149,600,000 km. What is the average distance from Mercury to the Sun?
    a. 5.8×10^6 km
    b. 5.8×10^7 km
    c. 3.9×10^6 km
    d. 0.39×10^6 km

Look at the Figure below, which shows a circle with center at point O and several line segments. Then, answer Questions 44-47.

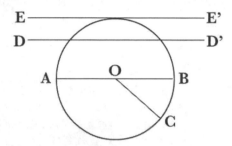

44. Which of the following represents the radius of the circle?
    a. EE'
    b. DD'
    c. AB
    d. OC

45. Line segment EE' is a
    a. diameter
    b. tangent
    c. secant
    d. chord

46. Line segment DD' is a
    a. radius
    b. secant
    c. chord
    d. diameter

47. If line segment AB is 6 cm in length, then the area of the circle is approximately
    a. 36 cm²
    b. 113 cm²
    c. 9 cm²
    d. 28 cm²

48. An elevator leaves the first floor of a 25-story building with 3 people on board. It stops at every floor. Each time it comes to an even-numbered floor, 3 people get on and one person gets off. Each time it comes to an odd-numbered floor, 3 people get on and 4 people get off. How many people are on board when it arrives at the 25th floor?

    a. 13
    b. 16
    c. 15
    d. 12

49. An old vinyl phonograph record is 12 inches in diameter. It rotates on a turntable at 33 revolutions per minute. What is the approximate linear speed of a fly sitting on the outer edge of the record?

    a. 21 inches per second
    b. 12 ½ inches per second
    c. 33 inches per second
    d. 16 inches per second

50. A shipping clerk can process 180 orders per hour. He has an assistant who can process 180 orders in 90 minutes. How many minutes will it take the two of them, working together, to process 115 orders?

    a. 36
    b. 23
    c. 27
    d. 30

Answer Explanations

Language Answers

1. C: One of the basic applications of the comma is to separate two sentences, or independent clauses. Both clauses of this sentence are independent, having both subject and verb, so it is appropriate to separate them with a comma.

2. C: Commas are used to set off introductory elements or phrases, such as "As a matter of fact".

3. D: A comma is not used to separate two clauses in a sentence if one of the clauses is dependent. In this sentence, the clause following the conjunction "but" lacks a subject and therefore depends upon the subject of the first clause.

4. C: Use the progressive form of a verb to indicate that an action that has started continued for some time or is still continuing. In this case, the tree began to grow when the watering increased, and is still growing. The simple past tense "grew" indicates that the action took place in the past and was completed or stopped happening.

5. B: The word in place of the blank must modify the verb "did". An adverb must be used to modify a verb, not an adjective. Of the choices presented, only "well" is an adverb. All the others are adjectives.

6. D: Since the tickets were given to the person referred to by the pronoun replacing the blank, the objective pronoun must be used. Choices A, B, and C are subjective pronouns that are used when the person referred to is the subject of the verb. Only "me" is in the objective case.

7. C: In choices A and B the subject is singular ("group" of "box"), so that a singular verb is called for, not the plural verb shown.

8. B: Choices A and C exhibit poor agreement between subject and verb, and choice D has an incorrect comma.

9. A: This is a simple declarative sentence with subject, verb and indirect object. Choices B and D lack a verb. Choice C does not require a comma.

10. C: In this sentence, an introductory clause is correctly set off by a comma. Choice A lacks parallel construction, since the act of renting a movie should be compared with the act of going to one, rather than with "excitement". Choice B has an unnecessary comma. Choice D should be broken into two sentences.

11. D: which is a simple imperative sentence. Choice A lacks a comma, Choice C has a comma where none belongs, and in Choice B the verb is in the wrong tense.
12. C: In a question, a comma can be used to set off the adverb "please." Choices A and B are not complete sentences. The apostrophe in Choice D does not belong there.

13. A: Choice B is slang. In Choice C, the semi-colon should be replaced by a comma. Choice D makes use of the wrong verb tense.

14. B: In this sentence, a parenthetical phrase is properly offset by commas. Choices A and C lack commas. Choice D improperly uses a negative verb.

15. B: In Choice A, the question mark should be outside of the quotation marks, since it is not part of the title. In Choice C, the title of the poem should be in quotation marks. Choice D should not use quotation marks since it is an indirect question.

16. D: In Choice A, "yen" should be offset by commas. Choice B lacks a verb and is not a complete sentence. Choice C should not have a question mark.

17. C: This is a compound sentence with one subject and two verbs. Choice A lacks a subject. The country name in Choice B requires no quotation marks.   A comma should be used to set off the subordinate clause at the beginning of Choice D.

18. A: The two sentences imply a cause and effect: spending $25,000 on the car has left the writer with insufficient funds for maintenance. Choice B implies the opposite causality.

19. B: Use of the conjunction "but" serves to emphasize the contrast between the two clauses: the success described in the first clause and the derision described in the second.

20. C: This choice makes explicit that the center fielder was rewarded because he broke the season record. Choice B suggests that breaking the record was itself a reward. Choice D suggests that he was being well rewarded (i e , well paid) even before breaking the record.

21. D: This choice makes it clear that the mechanic used the computer in order to perform the tests. Choice A makes the use of the computer appear incidental, while Choice C suggests that the mechanic was obliged to perform the tests because he used a computer.

22. A: This sentence introduces the concept of the letter of application that is developed in the remainder of the paragraph. Choice C is inappropriate since it describes both the letter and the resume: since the second sentence refers to "this letter", and not "the letter", it is clear that the first sentence must be about the letter alone.

23. C: This sentence clearly introduces the topic of the paragraph, which is the damage that may be sustained by library book collections as the result of an earthquake. Since deaths or injury are not discussed in the paragraph, Choices A and D are inappropriate. Also, the paragraph describes the types of damage that may occur, not specific damage that did occur during one earthquake, so that Choice B is inappropriate.

24. B: The remainder of the paragraph describes the differences between UVA and UVB rays. This sentence first tells the reader that these two types of ultraviolet ray exist, introducing the remainder of the text.

25. C: This paragraph describes checking accounts and their related services. Choice C continues that description by discussing ATM services and the charges that may accompany them. The other choices are also about banking, but they do not continue the description of checking account services.

26. A: This sentence, which suggests a visit in winter, leads naturally into the last sentence, which describes the weather conditions and wildlife activity at that time of year. The other choices are also about the Everglades, but bring up points that have nothing to do with the time of year.

27. D: This paragraph describes the law and the effects that it has had on the organic food market. Choice D follows the first sentence by beginning a description of the content of the law and leads naturally into the third sentence, which continues that description in more detail.

28. B: This sentence gives more information about tooth enamel, and explains why it is hard. The other choices are about teeth in general, but do not continue the discussion of tooth enamel.

29. C: This sentence gives more information about the accident that led to the sinking of the ferry. The other choices give information about the area, but they do not continue the theme of the ferry sinking that is introduced in the topic sentence.

30. B: This paragraph is about the Fortune magazine article on Getty and his answer to a question about his wealth. The information about the museum is unrelated to the other information presented in the paragraph and does not belong here.

31. B: This paragraph describes the use of vegetable oil as a diesel fuel, the problems involved in using it, and how to solve those problems with an engine conversion. The fact that there are many automobiles in the U.S. is not integral to this topic and does not belong in this paragraph.

32. A: Use of the conjunction "however" in this sentence contrasts the first and second clauses, showing the second to be a consequence of the first. Since the failure to find gold was unexpected, use of "then", as in Choice B, is inappropriate. In choice C, the conjunction should be followed by "so", to show that the second clause is a result of the first.

33. C: The adjective "egalitarian" means that all are considered to be equal. It is distinct from the adjective "democratic", which indicates a political system in which all have equal voting rights (Choice B). Choice A is slang, and "commensurate" in Choice D is nonsensical in this context.

34. D: The conjunction "although" contrasts the formation of a federation, which implies unity, with the development of border disputes. The federation could hardly have been caused by the border disputes, as implied in Choice A. Choices B and C simply string together the formation of the federation and the occurrence of the disputes without developing the relationship between them.

35. D: The phrase "Costa Rica's northern Guanacaste Province" constitutes the subject of this sentence and should not be set off by commas.

36. D: "Round" is a shape. "Around" means "in the vicinity", which is the phrase required here. Also, the comma is inappropriate in this compound sentence as the second verb does not have a separate subject.

37. B: In this sentence, a comma is used to set off an introductory phrase or word. The adjectival phrase "slightly larger than the size of the hole", which modifies the word "patch", should not be set off by commas or other punctuation.

38. C: The correct verb to use is "roughen", which means "to render something coarse". Since "area larger than the hole" is a phrase that must describe only the portion to be roughened, not the entire tube, Choice C is correct and Choice D is not.

39. B: The subject is in the third person, so use the contraction "doesn't" in place of "does not". Choices A and C, using the phrase "no more", are slang.

40. C: The two clauses are independent and should be separated by a comma. Since the sentence is imperative, there is no subject given for either clause.

41. A: The correct contraction is "you're", which is short for "you are". The word "your" is a possessive and is incorrect in this context. Additionally, the introductory word "now" should be offset by a comma.

42. B: It is necessary to use the adverb "heavily" rather than the adjective "heavy" to modify the verb. Also, the possessive form "Norway's" is called for, since "Norways" would be a plural and incorrect.

43. D: When separating the items of a list of 3 or more items with commas, use a comma after each item in the list. Note that Choice A changes the meaning of the sentence and indicates that the ships are made of metal.

44. C: Since the livestock comprises a portion of the diversified agriculture described by the sentence, the word "includes" provides the most precise meaning. The phrasings in the other choices are incorrect or awkward.

45. A: It is not the needs that are imported, but rather the foods to fill the needs. Choice D is incorrect because it uses the plural form "countries", rather than the possessive "country's".

46. C: The plural form "patients" must be used rather than the possessive. The present progressive form "are having" must be replaced by the simple present: "have" is acceptable, but the verb "experience" is more likely to be used in a medical diagnosis. The location of the pain is on the outside of the elbow, not "outside the elbow", which suggests it is outside of the body, entirely.

47. A: To radiate means to spread from the source. In this case the pain spreads from the elbow to the hand. Since this happens regularly, the simple present tense is called for.

48. B: This paragraph is written in the present tense, and so the tense of this sentence should be the same. Since the second clause is dependent, having no subject, it should not be set off by a comma, as it is in Choice C. Choice D contains an internal contradiction and makes no sense.

49. C: Choices A and B indicate that both men and women are affected, whereas the meaning of the original goes further: it tells us that both genders suffer the same effects. This is properly conveyed in choice C. Since the word "similarly" modifies the verb "affects", use the adverbial form as shown, not the adjective "same".

50. D: This paragraph is written in the present tense, and so the tense of this sentence should be the same. Choice A lacks a verb for the second clause and makes no sense. Choice B is slang and is less precise than the correct answer, Choice D.

51. B: The form in the original is slang. The present tense is called for in this paragraph, which is written in that tense. The forms in Choices C and D, which are in the future progressive, are also slang.

52. C: Use a colon to separate two clauses which could be separate sentences, but which are linked by some relationship in meaning. In the present usage (syntactical-deductive), the colon introduces a clause which describes a logical consequence of the preceding clause. The semi-colon may be used where such a logical consequence is not involved.

53. D: Commas may be used to set off a parenthetical clause which provides additional detail or modifies a component of the main sentence.

54. A: The original is a run-on sentence, with two completely independent clauses. Choice A breaks it cleanly into two separate sentences, which is the best way to correct it.

Reading Skill Answers

1. C: As stated in the second sentence of the second paragraph of the extract, motion studies seek to determine the most effective motion to accomplish a task, and they measure this by the amount of time the motion requires.

2. D: In the second paragraph, the text tells us that Lefevre was struck by the fact that, in traditional printing layouts, the letters used most often required the operator to reach farthest. In his new design, he corrected this.

3. A: The third paragraph describes Gilbreth's chronocyclegraph, which made photographs of lights that were attached to the wrists of his subjects.

4. C: This should be read from the column labeled "Unadjusted percent change to June 2009 from June 2008", a period of one year. For transportation, the index is down 13.2%. This is the only negative change among the choices given.

5. B: Read this answer in the second column from the right. Fuel oil and other fuels decreased by 3.1% during this period. Gasoline increased by 3.1%. The other commodities decreased, but by lesser amounts.

6. C: This should be read from the column labeled "Unadjusted percent change to June 2009 from May 2009", a period of one month. The number in this column of the table on the row corresponding to Food is a zero, indicating that there was no change in the price of food during this period.

7. D: In the table, components of each category are shown by indentation under the name of the category itself. There may be sub-categories within each category that are further indented. All of the Choices are indented under "Food at Home" except for "Alcoholic Beverages", which is a separate category.

8. A: Read this from the second column in the table, "Relative Importance December 2008". These numbers represent the average percentage of household budgets that are spent on the expenditure category. The greatest number, 43.421%, is on the row corresponding to housing.

9. B: The article informs the reader that most plastic food containers contain BPA, that BPA has been detected in stored foods, and that it is a material that may be toxic. Several alternative container types are listed to enable the reader to avoid containers with BPA.

10. D: The second paragraph tells us that, due to concern about its toxicity, Canada has banned the use of BPA, but not all plastics, in baby bottles. It has not banned the use of BPA in plastic products other than baby bottles, as suggested by Choice C.

11. C: While the author states that certain countries and states have banned BPA for these applications, he does not take a stand on this issue in the article. Nor is it suggested that stainless steel is the best material: it is merely listed as one of several alternatives. The author simply provides the reader with several different types of container that can be used.

12. A: According to the text, phthalates, including BPA, are used to soften plastics so that they may be molded. They do not make the plastics safer, nor do they permit the use of plastic containers in microwave ovens.

13. B: At the end of the text, the author provides a list of three ways to avoid potential problems with food storage containers. These involve selecting containers made of glass, stainless steel, or BPA-free plastics.

14. B: According to the text, canned foods have been found to be contaminated with BPA, because plastic liners are used in the cans. Since the author counsels the avoidance of BPA, he would most likely also recommend the avoidance of canned foods.

15. D: The text describes how the migratory patterns of these turtles move them around the entire Pacific. As a result, researchers from the Fish and Wildlife service were obliged to expand their conservation efforts beyond the beaches of California to encompass sites in the western Pacific as well.

16. B: The author refrains from trying to enlist the reader's efforts in work to protect the leatherbacks, and does not appear to seek support. Rather, the text is a factual report about the conservation efforts that are already taking place.

17. A: This can be inferred from the second paragraph, which says that it was thought that the California populations originated from "nearby" beaches. There is no mention in the text of a preference for warm waters and, if anything, the text implies that they swim extremely well. Finally, the text tells us that the various populations of leatherbacks are genetically identical.

18. D: At the end of the fifth paragraph, the author states: "Early results have inspired a cautious optimism: leatherback turtle populations seem to be recovering." This does not describe a rapid recovery, so Choice A is incorrect.

19. C: According to the author, "success of these conservation efforts will require a more complete understanding of the entire ecosystem in which the turtles live." The article goes on to state that this will necessitate "a broad approach that includes the restoration of feeding grounds, nesting beaches, and the migratory routes that connect them."

20. C: The article provides guidance for parents and guardians about educating children on the subject of money. After providing some background in the initial paragraphs, it ends with five paragraphs that suggest specific steps that can be taken for this purpose.

21. A: This is an example of a "hook", an introductory paragraph designed to intrigue the reader and encourage him to read further. Since most parents have experienced occasions when their child throws a tantrum in order to be given something he or she desires, they may wish to read on. The last sentence in this paragraph suggests that the relationship between money and a child's happiness is not so simple, and will be explored further in the text.

22. B: The article tells parents to take the time to explain the basics of money to their children. It tells us that children learn about money by observing their parents using it, and that parents should explain the reasons for their actions to children from an early age.

23. C: The author says that giving a child an allowance tied to the performance of certain family chores is an excellent way to teach the concept that money must be earned.

24. D: The author advises that, as children grow up and learn more, they should be allowed to make their own decisions about money and personal finances. Their decision-making should be supported with parental advice, but gradually the final decisions should be ceded to them.

25. A: The article provides information about a scheme to defraud internet users of money. It describes the mechanics of the fraud scheme and explains how the perpetrators intend to make money.

26. B: A *propensity* is a tendency to do something. Proclivity is a synonym for this. *Larceny* is a synonym for theft. Note that *pilferage* and *robbery* are also synonyms for theft, but that *talent,* which is a latent ability, does not mean the same thing as propensity, while *disinclination* has the opposite meaning.

27. B: According to the paragraph, the perpetrators cite many reasons for the need to send them money, among them payment of taxes, bribes to government officials, and legal fees.

28. D: Despite what might seem the unlikely nature of the come-on, according to the text the Nigerian letter scheme succeeds in bilking people out of millions of dollars annually.

29. D: A caricature is a picture that ludicrously exaggerates the defects of a thing or of a person. The author first mocks the Humboldt River for being so small, suggesting that it might be possible to drink the whole thing dry. He goes on to mock his own greed, with his exaggerated stalking of gold minerals.

30. A: Burlesque is a form of humor that makes use of ludicrous exaggeration. The description is obviously absurd and meant to exaggerate the inconveniences presented by the steep hillsides surrounding the town.

31. B: Mr. Ballou is described as "an experienced gold miner". His role in the passage is to provide a grounding in reality and to puncture the author's illusions about the ease of getting rich by finding gold.

32. B: In the final paragraph, the author compares gold and lower minerals such as mica to men of quality and lesser men, and bemoans the fact that they are just as hard to tell apart as are real gold and fool's gold, as illustrated by his story.

33. B: As set out in section 1.0, Purpose and Scope, the document describes a procedure for identifying hazards associated with one or more jobs (in this case Tank Operations) or encountered by visitors and for instituting controls to mitigate (or minimize) the dangers that they present.

34. D: The methods to be used to mitigate hazards are given in section 4.1 of the text, which indicates that they are specified in descending order of use. Protective clothing is an example of the last method listed, personal protective equipment, so this is the last strategy to be tried to protect the workers from the hazardous chemical.

35. D: Section 4.2 indicates that safety procedures ("controls") that fall within the scope of normal training for workers do not need to be discussed in the work instructions for operations that are performed frequently.

36. A: The document is intended as a guide for those writing work instructions for jobs to be performed at the site. These work instructions are prepared by management. Workers and laborers would read those documents as part of their training.

37. D: Section 4.5 indicates that safety procedures that are not within the qualification and training of the workers for hazards should have detailed instructions for how the workers are to mitigate the hazard.

38. B: The extract includes a number of plays on words, exaggerations, and other comic devices that show that it is meant to be funny.

39. C: As part of their argument, the Doctor and Martine are regretting that they are married to one another. As a result, she regrets the day that she said "yes, and, in the very next line, he regrets having signed the marriage papers.

40. A: In this section, Martine levels a series of accusations at the Doctor: drinking, selling the furniture, gambling. His answers are all flippant one-liners that mock her and that show no regret. Nor does he attempt to defend his actions in any way.

41. C: The Doctor drinks, gambles, sells all that they own and takes no responsibility for the children. He does not appear to be irascible or choleric (both indicate someone who is easily angered) or intolerant (someone who does not respect other beliefs or opinions).

42. D: In this portion of the extract, the Doctor tells Martine to be gentle and, backing away, tells her not to get into a passion, that is, to become emotional. He tries to placate her and then, in the last line, stands his ground and becomes combative as well.

43. C: The text indicates that all such information should be restricted to the resume, and that photocopies of book pages, for example, from which publication information could be deduced, are not acceptable.

44. D: The instructions state that applicants submitting excerpts must include a one-page statement in the manuscript about where it fits into the whole to orient the reviewers.

Mathematics Computation Answers

1. B: Set up the subtraction as shown, and subtract each digit beginning at the right:

$$
\begin{array}{r}
4.73 \\
-2.13 \\
\hline
2.60
\end{array}
$$

2. B: Isolate the variable, x, on the left side of the equation by subtracting 7 from each side. This leaves $x = 11 - 7 = 4$.

3. C: The 2 in the first number is in the hundredths position, and the 3 in the second number is in the ten-thousandths position. This is carried over into the sum. Set up the addition as follows and carry the digits down, adding them beginning at the right:

$$
\begin{array}{r}
1.02 \\
+0.0003 \\
\hline
1.0203
\end{array}
$$

4. D: 4 goes into 68 17 times. To see that this is true, multiply the result, 17, by 4:

$$
\begin{array}{r}
17 \\
\times\ 4 \\
\hline
68
\end{array}
$$

5. C: "Percent" means "parts per 100". Divide the number 19 by 100 and then multiply by 20 to obtain the result: $\frac{19}{100} = 0.19$; $0.19 \times 20 = 3.8$.

6. B: Since $0.3 = \frac{3}{10}$, the division is equivalent to $\frac{18}{4} \div \frac{3}{10}$. To divide by a fraction, multiply by its inverse. This gives $\frac{18}{4} \times \frac{10}{3} = \frac{180}{12} = \frac{45}{3} = 15$.

7. E: To divide a fraction by another fraction, multiply by the inverse. Following this procedure, $\frac{8}{7} \div \frac{12}{7} = \frac{8}{7} \times \frac{7}{12}$. The two numbers 7 will cancel, leaving $\frac{8}{12}$. This can be simplified by dividing both numerator and denominator by 4, leaving $\frac{2}{3}$ as the final answer. Since this is not one of the choices given, E is correct.

8. A: Perform the operation within the grouping symbols first. This yields $3 - 1 = 2$. Since $2^2 = 4$, the equation reduces to $4 - 4$, and this equals zero, or Choice A.

9. C: Since both the numerator and denominator are negative, the minus signs cancel. Consider that both are products of (- 1), so that the division is equivalent to $\frac{(-1)27}{(-1)3} = \frac{27}{3} = 9$.

10. B: The symbol shown is a *radical*, and calls for the square root of the number under the symbol, the *radicand*. The square root is a number which, multiplied by itself, yields the radicand. Since 6 x 6 = 36, Choice B is correct.

11. C: The product of zero and any other number is equal to zero. Conversely, if the product of two numbers is equal to zero, then at least one of those two numbers must be zero (zero product property).

12. D: Convert both mixed numbers to fractions with the same denominator, i.e., 8. Since 6 x 8 = 48, then $6\frac{5}{8} = \frac{48+5}{8} = \frac{53}{8}$. Also, since 3 x 8 = 24, then $3\frac{7}{8} = \frac{24+7}{8} = \frac{31}{8}$. Therefore, the addition becomes $6\frac{5}{8} + 3\frac{7}{8} = \frac{53}{8} + \frac{31}{8} = \frac{84}{8} = 10\frac{4}{8} = 10\frac{1}{2}$. Another way to add mixed numbers is to add the whole numbers and add the fractions, then combine the answers.
$6\frac{5}{8} + 3\frac{7}{8} = (6+3) + (\frac{5}{8} + \frac{7}{8}) = 9 + \frac{12}{8} = 9 + 1\frac{4}{8} = 10\frac{4}{8} = 10\frac{1}{2}$

13. D: The addition of a negative number is equivalent to the subtraction of that number, so that + (-4) is the same as – 4. The problem is therefore the same as 16 – 4 – 7. Subtracting each number in turn yields 16 – 4 = 12; 12 – 7 = 5, so that choice D is correct.

14. B: The 2 in the first number is in the thousandths position, the zero in the hundredths position, and the 3 in the tenths position. The 1 in the second number is in the hundredths position and the 7 in the tenths position. Set up the addition as follows and add like digits from the right, carrying over as necessary:
```
   4.302
+6.71
11.012
```

15. A: To subtract a negative number from another number, add its absolute value. The subtraction becomes 7.19 + 3.2 = 10.39.

16. C: Convert the fraction into decimal notation: $\frac{1}{4} = 0.25$. The addition becomes $8.65 + 0.25 = 8.90$.

17. D: 10% of 60 is 6. 50% (or one half) of 60 is 30. The sum of these 30 + 6 = 36 is therefore 50% + 10% = 60% of 60. Another way to see this is to divide $\frac{36}{60} = 0.6 = 60\%$.

18. C: First, isolate the variable on one side of the equal sign. This gives $\frac{1}{2}k = 9 - 6 = 3$. Next, multiply both sides of this equality by 2 to solve for k: $k = 2 \times 3 = 6$.

19. C: To divide two powers of the same number, subtract the exponents. The problem becomes $\frac{3^7}{3^5} = 3^{7-5} = 3^2 = 3 \times 3 = 9$.

20. E: Subtracting a negative number is equivalent to adding its absolute value, so the problem becomes 7 + 4 – 4 = 7. Since this is not one of the choices given, Choice E must be selected.

21. B: To add mixed numbers such as these, add the whole numbers and add the fractions separately. To add two fractions with the same denominator, add the numerators and retain the denominator. This gives $6 + 2 = 8$, and $\dfrac{3}{13} + \dfrac{4}{13} = \dfrac{7}{13}$. Since the fraction is less than 1, we need not simplify, and the answer is Choice B.

22. C: "Percent" means "parts per 100". Divide the number 1000 by 100 and then multiply by 30 to get 30%. This gives $1000 \times \dfrac{30}{100} = 300$.

23. A: To divide by a fraction, multiply by its inverse. This gives $\dfrac{8}{18} \div \dfrac{4}{18} = \dfrac{8}{18} \times \dfrac{18}{4} = \dfrac{8}{4} = 2$.

24. D: Since $0.9 = \dfrac{9}{10}$, the division may be performed by multiplying by the inverse of this fraction. This gives $81.09 \times \dfrac{10}{9} = \dfrac{810.9}{9}$. To perform this division mentally, note that $810 = 10 \times 81$, and that $81 = 9 \times 9$. Therefore, $\dfrac{810}{9} = \dfrac{9 \times 9 \times 10}{9} = 90$. To deal with the decimal, note that $\dfrac{0.9}{9} = \dfrac{1}{10} = 0.1$. Combining these two operations gives $90 + 0.1 = 90.1$.

25. D: The square of a number is equal to the product of the number and itself, so that $4^2 = 4 \times 4 = 16$. Since $16 + 4 = 20$, Choice D is correct. Choice A indicates the cube of the number, which is equal to the number multiplied by itself three times, or $4^3 = 4 \times 4 \times 4 = 64$.

26. A: To multiply two fractions, multiply the numerators and the denominators separately. In this case, for the numerators $7 \times 2 = 14$, and for the denominators $3 \times 3 = 9$. Combining yields $\dfrac{7}{3} \times \dfrac{2}{3} = \dfrac{14}{9}$.

27. C: The operation enclosed in the grouping symbols should be performed first. Since $6 - 4 = 2$, this yields $2 \times 2 = 4$.

28. D: Any number raised to the zero power is equal to 1. Since $6^0 = 1$, and $6^2 = 6 \times 6 = 36$, the problem is equivalent to $36 + 1 = 37$.

29. B: Since 23.01 is equivalent to 23.010, set up the subtraction as follows:
```
  23.010
- 2.999
  20.011
```

30. C: The operation in the grouping symbols should be performed first. Since $5 \times 20 = 100$, this reduces the problem to $\dfrac{100}{4} = 25$.

31. C: The operation in the grouping symbols should be performed first. Since $6 \times 3 = 18$, this reduces the problem to $-15 - 18$. To subtract a number from a negative number, add their absolute values and retain the negative sign. Thus, $-15 - 18 = -(15 + 18) = -33$.

32. A: Isolate the variable by adding 4 to both sides of the equation. This yields $x^2 = 36$. Now, take the square root of both sides of the equation to solve for x: $x = \sqrt{36} = 6$.

33. B: Convert the fractions so that they have the same denominators by multiplying both the numerator and denominator of the first fraction by 3. This gives $6\frac{3}{9} - 4\frac{2}{9}$. The whole numbers and fractions of the mixed numbers may now be subtracted independently. Since 6 – 4 = 2, and $\frac{3}{9} - \frac{2}{9} = \frac{1}{9}$, combining these yields $6\frac{1}{3} - 4\frac{2}{9} = 2\frac{1}{9}$.

34. B: "Percent" means "parts per 100". Setting the unknown number equal to x, this gives $\frac{30}{100}x = 18$. To solve this, isolate the variable by multiplying both sides of the equation by 100 and dividing both sides by 30, resulting in $x = (18)(\frac{100}{30}) = \frac{1800}{30} = 60$.

35. D: Since 9 x 9 = 81, $\sqrt{81} = 9$. Similarly, 5 x 5 = 25, and $\sqrt{25} = 5$.
Combining these yields 9 – 5 = 4.

36. A: Following normal order of operations, perform the multiplication before adding or subtracting terms that are not enclosed within grouping symbols. Since 7 x 2 = 14, the expression reduces to 6 – 14 – 1 = -9.

37. C: Perform the operation inside the grouping symbols first, then raise to the power indicated. Since 9 – 6 = 3, this equals $3^2 = 9$, and the expression reduces to 9 ÷ 9 = 1.

38. C: Perform the operation inside the grouping symbols first. This yields – 4 + 3 = - 1. Then, perform the multiplication. Since the product of two negative numbers is positive, this yields – 1 x – 12 = 12.

39. B: To divide by a fraction, multiply by its inverse. The problem becomes $\frac{85}{18} \div \frac{17}{18} = \frac{85}{18} \times \frac{18}{17} = \frac{85}{17} = 5$.

40. C: "Percent" means "parts per 100", so the problem can be re-stated as $\frac{23}{100} \times 10000 = 23 \times 100 = 2300$.

Applied Mathematics Answers

1. D: If Bob buys the paper every day for $1.50, in 7 days he will spend 7 x $1.50 = $10.50. If he subscribes, he spends only $3.50. Therefore, his savings is the difference $10.50 - $3.50 = $7.00.

2. B: Since $\frac{4}{5}$ of $\frac{5}{7}$ of 35 boys were at the practice, this is $35 \times \frac{5}{7} \times \frac{4}{5} = 35 \times \frac{4}{7} = 5 \times 4 = 20$.

3. C: Since an 18% tip was added, the amount paid was equal to 118% of the total before the tip was added. Therefore, that total is calculated as $\$1128.08 \times \frac{100}{118} = \$956.00$.

4. A: Point A is in the second quadrant, to the upper left of the origin, which is the point where the x- and y-axes cross one another. In this quadrant, x values are negative and y values are positive. When the coordinates of a point are given for a Cartesian graph such as this, the x-value is given first, the y-value second. So the given coordinates correspond to $x = -3, y = +4$. This corresponds to the position of point A in the second quadrant.

5. B: Read the coordinates of point C from the graph: it is at (-3, -3). That is, $x = -3$ and $y = -3$. Similarly, point A is at (-3, 4). Since the x-values are the same, the distance between the points is equal to the difference between the y-values: 4 – (-3) = 7.

6. C: First, measure the distance between points A and B. Read the coordinates of point B from the graph: it is at (4, 3). That is, $x = 4$ and $y = 3$. Similarly, point A is at (-3, 4). Since the y-values are the same, the distance between the points is equal to the difference between the x-values: 3 – (-3) = 6. The distance between points A and C is 7 units (Question 5). Since the figure is a rectangle, the total perimeter is equal to twice the sum of these distances, that is, 2 x (6 + 7) = 26.

7. B: Substitute each of the given values for x and y into the equation. This yields $(4)^2 - (2 \times 3 - 3) = 16 - 3 = 13$.

8. C: Write two equations to express the problem. Since the entertainment portion (E) lasted 15 minutes less than 4 times the advertising portion (A), the first equation is $E = 4A - 15$. Since both sections add up to the total show length, 60 minutes, the second equation is $E + A = 60$. Substituting the first equation into the second yields $4A - 15 + A = 60$, which is equivalent to 5A = 75. Dividing both sides of this equation by 5 shows that A = 15 minutes. Now, since $E + A$ = 60, it follows that E = 60 – 15 = 45 minutes.

9. A: This is an arithmetic sequence in which each term is equal to the preceding term plus (-3). To find the missing term, add (-3) to the preceding term: 15 + (-3) = 15 – 3 = 12. To verify this result, add (-3) to this term: this results in the following term: 12 + (– 3) = 12 – 3 = 9.

10. D: Two adjacent angles that form a straight line are called supplementary angles. In order to form a straight line, the sums of their measures must be 180°. Since the angle $\angle$**a** is equal to 70°, then $\angle$**b** = 180 – 70 = 110°.

11. C: When two parallel lines are intersected by a third straight line (called a transversal), the angles in matching corners are called corresponding angles and are congruent to one another. Lines $L1$ and $L2$ are parallel and are intersected by the transversal $L3$ to form corresponding angles $\angle a$ and $\angle i$. Since the measure of $\angle a$ is equal to 70°, then the measure of $\angle i$ must also be equal to 70°.

12. B: Angles $\angle n$ and $\angle p$ are corresponding angles for the transversal line $L2$ intersecting lines $L3$ and $L4$. If the corresponding angles are congruent, the lines must be parallel.

13. A: Angles $\angle a$ and $\angle c$ are corresponding angles and must be congruent. Angles $\angle c$ and $\angle k$ are corresponding angles and must be congruent. Therefore, $\angle a$ and $\angle k$ must be congruent. Furthermore, angles $\angle k$ and $\angle p$ are vertical angles (formed by two intersecting straight lines), so that $\angle k$ is congruent to $\angle p$. Similarly, $\angle a$ is congruent to $\angle f$. Therefore, all four angles are congruent to one another and statement A is true.

14. C: There are 200 possible outcomes to this experiment, one for each of the marbles in the jar. Each outcome is equally likely. Thirty of the possible outcomes are for a blue marble to be drawn. Therefore, the probability of this outcome is $\frac{30}{200} = 0.15 = 15\%$.

15. B: Thirty-six out of a total of 55 men received a grade of 75 or higher (24 + 12). The percentage of men with passing grades is calculated as $\frac{36}{55} \times 100 = 0.65 = 65\%$, approximately.

16. C: Thirty-four out of 118 total applicants received a grade of 85 or higher (32+2). The percentage is calculated as $\frac{34}{118} \times 100 = 0.29 = 29\%$, approximately.

17. B: Two women scored in the range 95 and above. None of the men did. So, at least these two women scored higher than any of the men. It is possible that some of the women who scored in the range 84 – 95 also scored higher than any of the men (if none of the men had scores at the top of this range), but it is not possible to show this from the data in the table.

18. A: Since 12 inches equals 1 foot, each tile is 1 square foot in area. The area of the bedroom floor is 15 x 18 = 270 square feet. Therefore, the number of tiles that must be laid is 270. Since Morgan can lay 9 tiles per hour, the time required will be $\frac{270}{9} = 30$ hours.

19. D: Tamara can pull any sock out the first time, since the color does not matter. For the second time, there is only one remaining sock out of 9 that matches the color of the sock she drew the first time, so the probability of drawing that one is $\frac{1}{9}$.

20. B: The average is the total number of seconds divided by the total number of events. If there are four events (four swimmers), the average will be $22 = \frac{Total}{4}$. Solving for the total yields $Total$ = 88 seconds. The total for the first three swimmers is 22.4 + 23.8 + 21.9 = 68.1 seconds. Therefore, the last swimmer must swim his lap in 88.0 – 68.1 = 19.9 seconds.

21. B: The scores for 2007 correspond to the grey bars. In 2007, school 3 had an average score of 46, lower than any of the others. It was the only school that experienced a decline in scores.

22. D: The change in reading scores corresponds to the difference between the white and grey bars for each school. School 5 scores increased from 51 to 55 over this interval, greater than the increase for any other school.

23. A: The scores for 2006 correspond to the white bars. The highest score for 2006 was obtained by school 2 and was a 52.

24. C: The cost for plan A is 1200 x $0.10 = $120; for plan B it is $50 + (600 x $0.12) = $122; for plan C it is $75 + (300 x $0.14) = $117; for plan D it is $100 + (200 x $0.18) = $136.

25. D: Substitute the given values into the expression, yielding $\frac{1}{3}(3)^2 + \frac{3 \times 4}{4} = 3 + 3 = 6$.

26. B: At 25 miles per gallon, Rouenna will need $\frac{500}{25} = 20$ gallons of gasoline. At $3 per gallon, this will cost 3 x 20 = $60.

27. C: To calculate the mean, or average, add the stock prices and divide by the number of stocks. This yields $\frac{127 + 21 + 24 + 193 + 30}{5} = 79$.

28. D: The median is the middle value of a group of numbers. In this case, there are two prices greater than 30, and two prices less than 30. Therefore, 30 is the middle value.

29. B: According to the chart, housing expenses average 48% of the total expenses for the American population. The next largest expense is food which, at 18%, is much lower.

30. B: Since clothing expenses are 8% of the total, on average, according to the chart, for a household spending $40,000 clothing would comprise 0.08 x 40,000 = $3,200.

31. D: Solve by setting up the cross product: $2x = (-3) \times 8 = -24$. Divide both sides of this equation by 2 to isolate the variable: $x = -12$.

32. A: To solve this problem, work backwards. Since there are 6400 yeast cells present at 3 hours and the culture doubles every half hour, there were 6400 x $\frac{1}{2}$ = 3200 cells present at 2.5 hours. At time $t = 0$, there were 6400 x $\frac{1}{2}$ x $\frac{1}{2}$ x $\frac{1}{2}$ x $\frac{1}{2}$ x $\frac{1}{2}$ x $\frac{1}{2}$ = 6400 x $\frac{1}{64}$ = 100 cells in the culture.

33. A: Let d represent the distance between the two towns. Then $\frac{d}{90}$ is the time it takes Mischa to drive the distance, and $\frac{d}{60}$ is the time it takes Brenda to drive the same distance. Since this is 3 hours longer

- 96 -

than Mischa's time, $\frac{d}{90} + 3 = \frac{d}{60}$. To solve this equation for d, first gather the terms with the variable on one side: $\frac{d}{60} - \frac{d}{90} = 3$. Isolate the variable to yield $d(\frac{1}{60} - \frac{1}{90}) = 3$. The least common multiple for the denominators is 180, so this is equivalent to $d\left(\frac{3-2}{180}\right) = \frac{d}{180} = 3$. This yields $d = 3 \times 180 = 540$ km.

34. C: The area of a triangle equals the height multiplied by one-half of the base. The base, BC, is also the width of the rectangle $BCED$. Since $Area = \frac{1}{2}h \times base$, solve for the base BC:

$base = \frac{2 \times Area}{h} = \frac{2 \times 240}{20} = 24$ cm. Since the height of the rectangle is twice the height h of the triangle, it is equal to 40 cm. The area of the rectangle is given by $Area = height \times base = 24 \times 40 = 960$ cm².

35. D: Triangles $\triangle ABC$ and $\triangle AFG$ are similar, since they share the angle at A and FG is parallel to BC. The height, H, of the larger triangle equals $3h$ (since the length BD of the rectangle is twice the height h of the smaller triangle). Since the triangles are similar, the base FG must be 3 times the base BC. Applying the formula for the area of a triangle yields $Area_{AFG} = \frac{1}{2}H \times FG = \frac{1}{2}(3h)(3 \times BC)$. Since the area of the smaller triangle is $Area_{ABC} = \frac{1}{2}h \times BC$, then $Area_{AFG} = 9 \times Area_{ABC} = 9 \times 240 = 2160$ cm².

36. B: Triangles $\triangle ABC$ and $\triangle AFG$ are similar, since they share the angle at A and FG is parallel to BC. The height, H, of the larger triangle equals $3h$ (since the length BD of the rectangle is twice the height h of the smaller triangle). Since the triangles are similar, the base FG must be 3 times the base BC. Since the triangles are isosceles, $\triangle CEG$ is congruent to $\triangle BFD$. Therefore $FD = EG$, and since $DE = BC$, it follows that $FD = BC$. The area of $\triangle BDF$ is $Area_{BFD} = \frac{1}{2}base \times height$. For this triangle, the base FD is the same as the base of $\triangle ABC$, or BC. The height, BD, is twice the height of $\triangle ABC$. Therefore, $Area_{BFD} = 2 \times Area_{ABC} = 2 \times 240 = 480$ cm².

37. C: Alfredo's weekly base is 40 x $20 = $800. This week he made $950 - $800 = $150 from overtime. At $30 per hour, this corresponds to $\frac{150}{30} = 5$ hours of overtime. Added to his normal workweek, he worked 40 + 5 = 45 hours in all.

38. D: This is a geometric series, in which a constant ratio is maintained between each term and the next. From the first two terms, for example, it can be seen that the ratio is $\frac{6}{3} = 2$. This holds for all other sequential terms. To calculate the next term in the series, multiply the preceding term by this ratio. This yields 24 x 2 = 48.

39. A: From the definition of the PE ratio, $\dfrac{Price}{Earnings \quad per \quad share} = 12$. Therefore, earnings per share must be equal to $\dfrac{Price}{12} = \dfrac{\$6.00}{12} = \$0.50$. Since there are 3 million shares issued, the total earnings must be $0.50 x 3,000,000 = $1.5 million.

40. C: To see that Choice A is incorrect, note that Saturn's mass is less than that of Jupiter, but its orbital period is longer. To see that Choice B is incorrect, note that Saturn's diameter is greater than that of Earth, but its gravity is less. To see that Choice D is incorrect, note that Saturn's mass is greater than that of Earth, but its gravity is less.

41. A: According to the table, the mass of Venus is 0.815 times that of Earth. Since 0.815 x 6 x 10^{24} = 4.9 x 10^{24}, Choice A is correct.

42. B: To see that Choice A is incorrect, note that Neptune's orbital period is greater than that of Jupiter, but its orbital speed is less. To see that Choice C is incorrect, note that Saturn's diameter is less than that of Jupiter, and its orbital speed is less. To see that Choice D is incorrect, note that Saturn's mass is greater than that of Earth, but its orbital speed is less.

43. B: In scientific notation, the distance 149,600,000 km is written as 1.496 x 10^8 km. According to the table, Mercury is 0.39 times as far from the Sun as is the Earth. Since 0.39 x 1.496 x 10^8 = 5.8 x 10^7, Choice B is correct.

44. D: The radius is a straight line segment reaching from the center of a circle to its circumference.
45. B: A tangent is a straight line that intersects the circumference of a circle at a single point.

46. B: A secant is a straight line that intersects the circumference of a circle at more than one point. Note that a chord is a line segment that extends from one point on the circumference to another.

47. D: The line segment AB is a diameter of the circle, since it passes through the center, O. The radius, R, of the circle is half the length of the diameter. Since AB = 6 cm, then R = 3 cm. The area of a circle is given by the formula $Area = \pi R^2 = \pi(3)^2 = 9 \times 3.14 = 28.26$.

48. B: There are 12 even-numbered floors between floors 1 and 25. At each one, the elevator gains 2 people, for a net gain of 24. There are 11 odd-numbered floors between floors 1 and 25 (not counting floors 1 and 25). At each one, the elevator loses 1 person, for a net loss of 11. The elevator leaves the first floor with 3 people, so the total arriving at the 25th floor is 3 + 24 – 11 = 16.

49. A: The radius, R, of the record is one half the diameter, or 6 inches. The circumference is given by $2\pi R$, which is 37.7 inches. Therefore, the fly rotates at 33 x 37.7 = 1244 inches per minute. Since there are 60 seconds in a minute, this is equivalent to $\dfrac{1244}{60} = 20.73$, or approximately 21 inches per second.

50. B: At 180 orders per hour, the clerk processes 3 orders per minute, since there are 60 minutes in an hour ($\frac{180}{60} = 3$). His assistant processes 2 orders per minute ($\frac{180}{90} = 2$). Together, they can process $3 + 2 = 5$ orders per minute. Therefore, 115 orders will take $\frac{115}{5} = 23$ minutes.

Special Report: TABE Secrets in Action

Sample Question from the English section

Louisa May Alcott's _____ the philosophical brilliance of her father's intellect was _____ by her impatience with his unworldliness

A.   exasperation with . . contradicted

B.   concealment of . . supplanted

C.   respect for . . augmented

D.   rebellion against . . qualified

E.   reverence for . . tempered

Let's look at a couple of different methods of solving this problem.

1. Understand What to Expect

Before you have read any of the answer choices and begin to stumble over some of the complicated vocabulary words used in the answer choices, see if you can predict what the answer might be, based on the information provided to you in the problem sentence. You aren't trying to guess the exact word that might be in the correct answer choice, but only the type of word that you should expect. Is it a positive word, negative word, etc.

Ask yourself what sort of words would likely fill the blanks provided. Consider the first blank, which comes directly before a description of the intellectual brilliance of Louisa's father. It is likely that she loved her father and thought highly of him, particularly with regards to his intelligence. Therefore, you should expect a verb with a positive meaning to fill the first blank.

The second blank comes directly before a description of her impatience with her father over his unworldliness. Her father's brilliance is a positive attribute, the unworldliness is a negative. The missing word is a verb that allows a transition between these two, somehow reconciling the positive and negative aspects of her father's character.

Now that you have an idea of what to expect in a correct answer choice, review the choices provided. Choices C and E both have a positive word to fill the first blank, "respect" and "reverence" respectively, so either could be correct. Moving to the second word to clarify which is the correct answer, you encounter the words "augmented" and "tempered". Augmenting deals with increasing or supporting. It doesn't make sense that a positive attribute of her father's would increase her impatience, making choice C incorrect. Tempering deals with modifying or adjusting. It does make sense that her perception of a positive attribute of her father's would be modified or adjusted by a negative attribute, making choice E correct.

2. Group the Answers

Review the answer choices and try to identify the common aspects of each answer choice. Are any of the words synonyms or antonyms?

Without ever having looked at the problem, but simply reviewing the answer choices can tell you a lot of information. Classify the words in the answer choice as positive or negative words and group them together. For example, you can tell that both answer choice A and D deal with "anger", using the words "exasperation" and "rebellion". Answer choices C and E deal with "appreciation", using the words "respect" and "reverence". Answer choice B stands alone, and in many cases can be immediately eliminated from consideration.

Grouping answers makes it easy to accept or reject more than one answer at a time. By reviewing the context of the sentence, "appreciation" makes more sense than "anger" in describing a woman's perception of her father's intellectual brilliance. Therefore, answer choices A and D can both be rejected simultaneously. Because "appreciation" is a likely description of Louisa's perception of her father's brilliance, choice B can be dismissed temporarily. If on further inspection answer choice C and E do not continue to make sense, then you can easily return to choice B for consideration.

Once again, in comparing the remaining words in choice C and E, "augmented" and "tempered", the meaning of the root word "temper" as a modifying agent makes it the better answer, and choice E correct.

3. Make it Easier

As you go through and read the sentence and answer choices, don't allow a complicated wording to confuse you. If you know the meaning of a phrase and it is over complicated, be sure to mentally substitute or scratch through and write above the phrase an easier word that means the same thing.

For example, you can rewrite "Louisa May Alcott's -------- the philosophical brilliance of her father's intellect was ------- by her impatience with his unworldliness" as "Louisa May Alcott's ---- her father's intelligence was   by her impatience with his simplicity.

Using words that are simpler and may make it easier for you to understand the true context of the sentence will make it easier for you to identify the correct answer choice. Similarly, you can use synonyms of difficult words as a mental replacement of the words in the answer choices to make it easier for you to understand how the word fits into the sentence.

For example, if you know the meaning of the word "supplanted" in choice B, but have difficulty understanding how it fits into the sentence, mentally replace it with the word "displaced." Displaced means the same thing and may be easier for you to read and understand in the context of the sentence.

Sample Question from the Mathematics Section

For a certain board game, two dice are thrown to determine the number of spaces to move. One player throws the two dice and the same number comes up on each of the dice. What is the probability that the sum of the two numbers is 9?

A. 0

B. 1/6

C. 2/9

D. 1/2

Let's look at a few different methods and steps to solving this problem.

1. Create an Algebra Problem

While you might think that creating an algebra problem is the last thing that you would want to do, it actually can make the problem extremely simple.

Consider what you know about the problem. You know that both dice are going to roll the same number, but you don't know what that number is. Therefore, make the number "x" the unknown variable that you will need to solve for.

Since you have two dice that both would roll the same number, then you have "2x" or "two times x". Since the sum of the two dice needs to equal nine, that gives you "2x = 9".

Solving for x, you should first divide both sides by 2. This creates 2x/2 = 9/2. The twos cancel out on the left side and you are have x = 9/2 or x = 4.5

You know that a dice can only roll an integer: 1, 2, 3, 4, 5, or 6, therefore 4.5 is an impossible roll. An impossible roll means that there is a zero possibility it would occur, making choice A, zero, correct.

2. Run Through the Possibilities for Doubles

You know that you have to have the same number on both dice that you roll. There are only so many combinations, so quickly run through them all.

You could roll:

Double 1's = 1 + 1 = 2
Double 2's = 2 + 2 = 4
Double 3's = 3 + 3 = 6
Double 4's – 4 + 4 – 8
Double 5's = 5 + 5 = 10
Double 6's = 6 ⎸ 6 = 12

Now go through and see which, if any, combinations give you a sum of 9. As you can see here, there aren't any. No combination of doubles gives you a sum of 9, making it a zero probability, and choice A correct.

3. Run Through the Possibilities for Nine

Just as there are only so many possibilities for rolling doubles, there are also only so many possibilities to roll a sum of nine. Quickly calculate all the possibilities, starting with the first die.

If you rolled a 1 with the first die, then the highest you could roll with the second is a 6. Since 1 + 6 = 7, there is no way that you can roll a sum of 9 if your first die rolls a 1.

If you rolled a 2 with the first die, then the highest you could roll with the second is a 6. Since 2 + 6 = 8, there is no way that you can roll a sum of 9 if your first die rolls a 2.

If you rolled a 3 with the first die, then you could roll a 6 with your other die and have a sum of 9. Since 3 + 6 = 9, this is a valid possibility.

If you rolled a 4 with the first die, then you could roll a 5 with your other die and have a sum of 9. Since 4 + 5 = 9, this is a valid possibility.

If you rolled a 5 with the first die, then you could roll a 4 with your other die and have a sum of 9. Since 5 + 4 = 9, this is a valid possibility.

If you rolled a 6 with the first die, then you could roll a 3 with your other die and have a sum of 9. Since 6 + 3 = 9, this is a valid possibility.

Now review all the possibilities that give you a combination of 9. You have: 3 + 6, 4 + 5, 5 + 4, and 6 + 3. These are the only combinations that will give you a sum of 9, and none of them are doubles. Therefore, there is a zero probability that doubles could give you a sum of 9, and choice A is correct.

4. Calculate the Odds

Quickly calculate the odds for just rolling a 9, without setting any restrictions that it has to be through doubles or anything else. You've seen in Method 3 that there are 4 ways that you can roll a sum of 9. Since you have two dice, each with 6 sides, there are a total of 36 different combinations that you could roll (6*6 = 36). Four of those thirty-six possibilities give you a sum of 9. Four possibilities of rolling a 9 out of thirty-six total possibilities = 4/36 = 1/9. So that means there is a 1/9 chance that would roll a 9, without any restrictions. Once you add restrictions, such as having to roll doubles, then your odds are guaranteed to go down and be less than 1/9. Since the odds have to be less than 1/9, the only answer choice that satisfies that requirement, is choice A, which is zero, making choice A correct.

Sample Question from the English Section

Alice Fletcher, the Margaret Mead of her day, assisted several American Indian nations that were threatened with removal from their land to the Indian Territory. She helped them in petitioning Congress for legal titles to their farms. When no response came from Washington, she went there herself to present their case.

According to the statement above, Alice Fletcher attempted to:

A. imitate the studies of Margaret Mead

B. obtain property rights for American Indians

C. protect the integrity of the Indian Territory

D. persuade Washington to expand the Indian Territory

Let's look at a couple of different methods of solving this problem.

1. Identify the key words in each answer choice. These are the nouns and verbs that are the most important words in the answer choice.

A. imitate, studies

B. obtain, property rights

C. protect, integrity

D. persuade, expand

Now try to match up each of the key words with the passage and see where they fit. You're trying to find synonyms between the key words in the answer choices and key words in the passage.

A. imitate – no matches; studies – no matches

B. obtain – no matches; property rights – matches with "legal titles" in sentence 2.

C. protect – no matches; integrity – no matches

D. persuade – matches with "petitioning" in sentence 2; expand – no matches

At this point there are only two choices that have any matches, choice B and D, and they both have matches with sentence 2. This is a good sign, because TABE will often write two answer choices that are close. Having two answer choices pointing towards sentence 2 as containing the key to the passage (and no other answer choices pointing to any other sentences) is a strong indicator that sentence 2 is the most likely sentence in which to find the answer.

Now let's compare choice B and D and the unmatched key words. Choice B still has "obtain" which doesn't have a clear match, while choice D has "expand" which doesn't have a clear match. To get into the mindset of Alice Fletcher, ask yourself a quick series of questions related to sentence 2.

Sentence 2 states "She helped them in petitioning Congress for legal titles to their farms."

Ask yourself, "Why did she do that?"

Answer: The American Indian nations wanted legal title to their farms and didn't already have it.

Then ask yourself: "So what did Alice Fletcher do?"

Answer: "She tried to help them get the legal title to their farms they wanted."

Now you've suddenly got that match. "Obtain" matches with "get", so your above answer could read, "She tried to help them get (or obtain) the legal title to their farms they wanted."

2. Use a process of elimination.

A. imitate the studies of Margaret Mead – Margaret Mead is only mentioned as a point of historical reference. The passage makes no mention of Mead's studies, only that Alice Fletcher is similar to her.

B. obtain property rights for American Indians – The passage discusses how American Indians were threatened with removal from their land, but Alice Fletcher helped them get legal title, going all the way to Washington to press their case. This is the correct answer. "Obtain property rights for American Indians" is exactly what she fought for.

C. protect the integrity of the Indian Territory – Protecting the integrity of a territory or area deals with maintaining a status quo of a boundary or border. Yet boundaries and borders aren't even mentioned in this passage, only property rights. It wasn't a boundary that Alice Fletcher was fighting to maintain, but rather the right for the American Indians to even live on the land at all.

D. persuade Washington to expand the Indian Territory – At first, this sounds like a good answer choice. Alice Fletcher was trying to persuade Washington. The difference though is that she wasn't trying to persuade them to expand the Indian Territory but legitimize it, i.e. grant legal title. "Expand" suggests dealing with an increase in square mileage, not the ownership at stake – remember the American Indians were threatened with removal from the land, not fighting to increase the amount of land under their control.

Sample Question from the English section

Sentence Correction Problem – Choose which of four ways of rewriting the sentence is correct.

As a consumer, one can accept the goods offered to us or we can reject them, but we cannot determine their quality or change the system's priorities.

A. As a consumer, one can accept
B. We the consumer either can accept
C. Either the consumer accepts
D. As consumers, we can accept

Let's look at a couple of different methods and steps to solving this problem.

1. Agreement in Pronoun Number

All pronouns have to agree in number to their antecedent or noun that they are representing. In the underlined portion, the pronoun "one" has as its antecedent the noun "consumer".

Go through and match up each of the pronouns in the answer choices with their antecedents.

A. consumer, one – correctly matches singular antecedent to singular pronoun
B. We, consumer – incorrectly matches plural antecedent to singular pronoun
C. consumer – no pronoun
D. consumers, we – correctly matches plural antecedent to plural pronoun

Based on pronoun number agreement, you can eliminate choice B from consideration because it fails the test.

2. Parallelism

Not only do the pronouns and antecedents in the underlined portion of the sentence have to be correct, but the rest of the sentence has to match as well. The remainder of the sentence has to be parallel to the underlined portion. In part of the sentence that is not underlined is the phrase "we can reject them," and another phrase, "but we cannot determine." Notice how both of these phrases use the plural pronoun "we". This means that the underlined portion of the sentence has to agree with the rest of the sentence and have matching plural pronouns and nouns as well.

Quickly review the answer choices and look for whether the nouns and pronouns in the answer choices are singular or plural.

A. consumer, one – singular noun and singular pronoun
B. We, consumer – plural pronoun and singular noun
C. consumer – singular noun
D. consumers, we – plural noun and plural pronoun

Only choice D has both a plural noun and a plural pronoun, making choice D correct.

Sample Question from the Mathematics Section

Table 1

Length of 0.10 mm diameter aluminum wire(m)	Resistance (ohms) at 20° C
1	3.55
2	7.10
4	14.20
10	35.50

Based on the information in Table 1, one would predict that a 20 m length of aluminum wire with a 0.10 mm diameter would have a resistance of:

A. 16 ohms

B. 25 ohms

C. 34 ohms

D. 71 ohms

Let's look at a few different methods and steps to solving this problem.

1. Create a Proportion or Ratio

The first way you could approach this problem is by setting up a proportion or ratio. You will find that many of the problems on the TABE can be solved using this simple technique. Usually whenever you have a given pair of numbers (this number goes with that number) and you are given a third number and asked to find what number would be its match, then you have a problem that can be converted into an easy proportion or ratio.

In this case you can take any of the pairs of numbers from Table 1. As an example, let's choose the second set of numbers (2 m and 7.10 ohms).

Form a question with the information you have at your disposal: 2 meters goes to 7.10 ohms as 20 meters (from the question) goes to which resistance?

From your ratio: 2m/7.10 ohms = 20m/x
"x" is used as the missing number that you will solve for.

Cross multiplication provides us with 2*x = 7.10*20 or 2x = 142.

Dividing both sides by 2 gives us 2x/2 = 142/2 or x = 71, making choice D correct.

2. Use Algebra

The question is asking for the resistance of a 20 m length of wire. The resistance is a function of the length of the wire, so you know that you could probably set up an algebra problem that would have 20 multiplied by some factor "x" that would give you your answer.

So, now you have 20*x = ?

But what exactly is "x"? If 20*x would give you the resistance of a 20 meter piece of wire, than 1*x would give you the resistance of a 1 meter piece of wire. Remember though, the table already told you the resistance of a 1 meter piece of wire – it's 3.55 ohms.

So, if 1*x = 3.55 ohms, then solving for "x" gives you x = 3.55 ohms.

Plugging your solution for "x" back into your initial equation of 20*x = ?, you now have 20*3.55 ohms = 71 ohms, making choice D correct.

3. Look for a Pattern

Much of the time you can get by with just looking for patterns on problems that provide you with a lot of different numbers. In this case, consider the provided table.

    1 – 3.55
    2 – 7.10
    4 – 14.20
    10 – 35.50

What patterns do you see in the above number sequences. It appears that when the number in the first column doubled from 1 to 2, the numbers in the second column doubled as well, going from 3.55 to 7.10. Further inspection shows that when the numbers in the first column doubled from 2 to 4, the numbers in the second column doubled again, going from 7.10 to 14.20. Now you've got a pattern, when the first column of numbers doubles, so does the second column.

Since the question asked about a resistance of 20, you should recognize that 20 is the double of 10. Since a length of 10 meant a resistance of 35.50 ohms, then doubling the length of 10 should double the resistance, making 71 ohms, or choice D, correct.

4. Use Logic

A method that works even faster than finding patterns or setting up equations is using simple logic. It appears that as the first number (the length of the wire) gets larger, so does the second number (the resistance).

Since the length of 10 (the largest length wire in the provided table) has a corresponding resistance of 35.50, then another length (such as 20 in the question) should have a length greater than 35.50. As you inspect the answer choices, there is only one answer choice that is greater than 35.50, which is choice D, making it correct.

Special Report: How to Find a Great Job in a Horrible Economy

If you've been laid off, or if you're in an industry where layoffs are possible, you really need to be thinking ahead of the curve. Get a job now in a safe industry while the getting is good and before the market is flooded with applicants. What are the most vulnerable industries? Take a look at the list below:

The Most Vulnerable Industries in a Downturn

- **Airlines and transportation**- in a slow economy, fewer goods are sold, business activity stalls or declines, and those who operate on the edge of growth and economic activity are exceptionally vulnerable. Most business travel can be postponed or done with increasingly sophisticated technology that makes travel somewhat obsolete. This makes the bread-and-butter of the airlines a very risky bet. The "premium" airlines that rely on juicy business rates are the riskiest- American Airlines, Delta, etc. Smaller economy airlines such as Southwest and Air Tran are better bets.

- **Manufacturers and marketers of durable goods**- a "durable good" is any purchase that can be postponed for a time during a budget crunch. Think about it- if you've just been laid off, buying a car or new refrigerator is not your first priority. Also, as bankruptcies increase, the amount of "good credit" will decline, meaning that large purchases that are often financed will be delayed until the purchaser has enough cash. Be prepared if your job depends on the success of a GM, Ford, Sears, Home Depot, or Pottery Barn.

- **Retailers in general**- excluding the deep discount chains like Wal-mart who will be the first to squeeze suppliers and cut costs in a bad economy, most retailers will suffer tremendously. Malls in particular have a glut of capacity, as this premium retail space has expanded at 3 times the rate of population growth for over 10 years straight! This is a warning for those needing Dillard's, Macy's, Restoration Hardware, or any mid-to-high end retailer to stay in business for them to keep their job.

- **Construction Industry**- any company conducting business in, or providing supplies to, the construction industry and or supporting the continued growth of production capacity.

If households delay buying a $20,000 car in a recession, what do you think they will do regarding a $300,000 mansion? Even more critically, what about companies considering a multi-million dollar new facility? Construction industries operate on the very margin of increased growth and capacity, and even the mildest recessions can send real estate and building material prices down the gutter. If commodity prices fail to fall as fast as demand for construction (all indications are that commodities will continue to fall, albeit at a slower pace since they have fallen so far already in the 90's), then suppliers of construction materials will be "squeezed" into bankruptcy within months. Beware of dependence on companies like Owens Corning, Lowe's, Centex, lumber companies, Square D, and firms with highly leveraged investments in real estate.

Stable and Predictable Industries in ANY Economy

The companies we're about to list are the best of both worlds: if the economy is good, you can take your paycheck and share in the wealth through the stock market; if the economy is bad, well at least you still have a paycheck!

- **Food and Beverage**- Proctor and Gamble, Frito-Lay, Kraft, Nestle, Post General Mills, Kellogg, Coke, etc. Sure, there are generics on the market, but people tend to make their most irrational economic decisions on small purchases- like paying 70% more for Hershey's brand cocoa that was packaged with the same commodity cocoa as the generic stuff. Not only that, these companies have managed to achieve a markup so astronomically high relative to raw material costs (the packaging of Corn Flakes is more expensive than the product!) that they can easily absorb increased price elasticity- it might not be good for their profit growth or stock price, but they won't go bankrupt either.

- **Beer and Cigarettes**- if you have an ethical problem with these companies, we completely respect that. Even so, these are probably the best industries for surviving a **depression**, not to speak of a recession. People buy alcohol and nicotine in any economy, and these companies show an unmatched record for consistent growth- meaning opportunities for not only continued employment but also genuine promotions and

- 116 -

professional development. Companies like: Phillip Morris, RJ Reynolds, Anheuser-Busch, Coors, Miller, etc.

o **Low Priced Consumable Essentials**- Ditto the same explanation as food and beverage- high margins, generics are not significant because of low price, and people have to buy them- stuff like toothpaste, razors, air filters, moisturizer, etc. Companies like Proctor and Gamble, Johnson and Johnson, Gillette, etc. The nice thing about working for a good "brand" is that the brand and products will likely survive a bankruptcy as long as the business model is still valid, of course under different ownership. An even better idea might be working for a manufacturer of generic rip-offs of brand name products- that's probably a growth industry, though not enough to bring the brands down entirely.

Growth Industries in a Recession or Depression

o **Outgrowths of the Economic Environment**- in a bankruptcy, the lawyers get paid first, and then the creditors, then finally the shareholders- the employees, of course, get nothing. However, before there can be a bankruptcy, there has to be a collections agent and a team of bankruptcy attorneys. This could be a HUGE growth industry, as the supply of specialists in collections (especially collections from white-collar debtors, not just deadbeats who missed a weekly payment on their TV) and bankruptcy specialists is far less than the possible demand. If you have the resources, go to law school and become a bankruptcy lawyer. Or, go to work for a collections agency at minimum wage until you learn the ropes, and then start your own practice. This may be THE self-employment opportunity of the decade.

o **Health Care**- the largest American generation in history, the Baby Boomers, ticks toward retirement every day. An older population means more medical care, more surgery, and more prescription drugs. Find a job in this field, and you will literally be set for life with job security. The possibilities are wide open- go to work for a manufacturer, work for a hospital, a nursing home, anything that will possibly increase in demand with an aging population. People will give their bottom dollar for their health, so this industry is as recession-proof as it gets.

We highly recommend that you give primary consideration to any job offer from the safe or growth industries. Such an offer is worth at LEAST 20% less salary than an offer in a risky business. The key to surviving an economic downturn is to maintain employment and keep developing yourself so you can fetch top dollar when things turn up- even during the Great Depression, 70% of the workforce was employed; **make sure you're in that 70%.**

Special Report: Are You Too Smart for Your Current Job?

Did you know that the best predictor of job performance is not a college diploma, not an interview, and not even grades or experience? Excluding past work performance, the best predictor of future work performance is a quality psychologists call "the g-factor:" general intelligence.

You may be wondering if you have "what it takes" for a certain profession: maybe a lawyer, doctor, engineer, or accountant. While intelligence doesn't explain everything (and certainly doesn't account for the vital necessities of a work ethic, motivation, and drive to succeed), all else being equal, it gives you the best measure of how you would stack up against others in a given field.

The number associated with intelligence is the Intelligence Quotient, or I.Q. The average for Americans is 100, and the standard deviation is 15. Standard deviation is a statistical term meaning, in plain language, "the typical distance from the average of the typical person." For example, though the average is 100, very few people have the exact IQ of 100. Because of the way it is computed, a person with a 115 IQ (the average plus one standard deviation) is in the 84th percentile of intelligence, smarter than 84% of the general population. Likewise, someone with an 85 IQ is in the 16th percentile.

How can you use this information? Simple- take an IQ test and determine your own IQ, and then compare your own IQ to that of the average person in your profession. If you are more than 15 points higher than the average person in your profession, you are probably too smart for your job, and would be better off in a higher IQ career! Your best bet is to research careers where you are above average but not by more than 15 points.

Here's a source for a free IQ test online:
http://www.emode.com/tests/uiq/

On the following table you will find the average IQ's of various professions:

Occupation	Average IQ
Professor/Researcher	133
Physician	128
Lawyer	128
Engineer	125
Teacher	122
General Managers	122
Nurses	119
Salesperson	114
Electrician	109
Foreman	109
Police	108
Mechanic	106
Machine Operators	105
Pipe Fitters	98

You can usually estimate the IQ of your own profession by comparing the complexity of the typical job at your pay rate (not necessarily YOUR job, since if you're smarter than average the company may be taking advantage of you by giving you harder work for the same pay) to the complexity of the above jobs. For example, accounting is more complicated than teaching or general management, but less complicated than engineering: reasonably, accountants probably have a mean IQ of about 123-124; of course, exact numbers aren't important in a statistical tool, since it only reflects a general trend, not the characteristics of every single accountant (in fact, nearly all will be significantly higher or lower than the average).

A practical example: If you're an administrative assistant with a 150 IQ, both you and society would see a greater benefit if you became a doctor or professor. Once you know your capabilities, make the most of them by considering jobs where you will be challenged to your fullest potential.

Special Report: Four Opportunities for Getting a Job NOW

Opportunity #1 – Nursing

Nursing is a wide-open field with great professional opportunities and high-income potential- here's the best part- they're BEGGING for people to become nurses. Nurses are much more than hospital maids or assistants, they are highly educated professionals whose practical functional knowledge of the human body and health compares to the theoretical knowledge possessed by a doctor. Here's what we like best about nursing- you get paid by the hour, including overtime and often double and triple time for holidays and call-ins! In a 40-hour week, a registered nurse will make about $40,000 a year- if they work 50 hours like the typical corporate salaried employee (who doesn't get paid anything for overtime), they rake in over $55,000 a year. Nurse practitioners working 50 hours make over $80,000 a year! To find out more about nursing, we recommend the following website:

http://www.discovernursing.com

Opportunity #2 – Military Officer

The military is always hiring. If you are under 27 and have a college degree (esp. if you are single), life as a military officer can be fun and rewarding. Military officers start at about $30,000 a year, and pay increases to over $50,000 very quickly- not only that, but the perks are unbelievable- paid food, housing, clothing, 30 days of paid vacation a year, tax-free shopping in non-profit stores, free travel, and full pension and retirement with lifetime health benefits after just 20 years of service. If you're 25 now, you could completely retire by age 45. We hear the Air Force treats their people best, followed by the Coast Guard, Navy, Marine Corps, and Army; one advantage of The Army is that they do not necessarily require a college degree for an officer commission, just a high enough test score on their recruiting test. All equivalent ranks get the same pay in all services. See the following sources for Armed Forces opportunities in the US:

http://www.af.mil

http://www.army.mil

http://www.navy.mil

http://www.uscg.mil

http://www.usmc.mil

Opportunity #3 – Teaching Under Alternative Certification

Most states now offer some sort of alternative certification for teachers. What this means is that anyone with a college degree can go to a two week "teaching boot camp" and be in a classroom immediately after (with full pay). States are hurting for new teachers, as most current teachers will retire in the near future. The pay is better than people realize (as you only work 10 out of 12 months), the hours can be reasonable, and the benefits and retirement packages of most states are quite generous. Not only that, but you'll make a real difference too. More information about teaching and alternative certification can be found here:

http://www.alt-teachercert.org

Opportunity #4 - Post 9/11 Federal Law Enforcement

The Feds are hiring, and don't think you have to sit behind a gray desk in Washington to get in on this opportunity. The most exciting opportunity in FedLand right now is with the US Border Patrol. You'll be protecting American jobs and security while earning a good paycheck in the CHEAPEST place to live in the country- along the US-Mexico border. We even hear they are offering signing bonuses for all comers, whether professional or operational (college degree and non-degreed positions). More information can be found here:

http://www.ins.usdoj.gov/graphics/workfor/careers/bpcareer/index.htm

Special Report: An Actual Top-Secret Corporate Interview File

The following pages reveal an actual behavioral interview guide used by interviewers and job recruiters at major US corporations. Read over the guide and you will see what the person sitting on the other side of the desk is using to "grade" your interview performance. By understanding the process, you will eliminate some of the unknown and be better prepared.

The interview form begins on the next page.

Behavioral-Based Interview Questions

When conducting job interviews, it is important to ask questions not only about an applicant's job knowledge and skills, but also of past work experiences. In particular, it is valuable to gather information in order to reveal how the applicant behaved in certain work situations. The applicant's past behavior often predicts how he/she will respond in similar future situations.

This information is important because how an employee behaves in completing responsibilities is as critical as what the responsibilities are in the actual job. Identifying and assessing required key behaviors should contribute to the overall success of an employee in their position.

Prior to asking the behavioral interview questions, it is recommended to begin the interview with general introductory questions. The following are offered as suggestions:

- Please highlight your past jobs telling me the employment dates when you worked for companies and what your job duties were (candidate should not have resume in hand, they should be able to recite from memory). If there are any gaps in employment, inquire about the situation(s).

- I have reviewed your resume but would like to ask you to begin by giving me an overview of your education and experience as they relate to this position and why you are interested in this position.

- Please elaborate on one of the work experiences listed on your resume.

- What were your major responsibilities?

- What were some of the most difficult duties of that job?

- Who did you report to and who reported to you (title)?

- What special skills and knowledge were needed to perform the duties in your previous jobs?

- Your resume/application lists many job changes. Tell me about that.

- How has your present/previous job changed while you've held it?

- What unique talent do you offer? Why do you feel it is unique?

- What else should I know about your qualifications for this job?

Organizational Success

Teamwork/Cooperation

- Gaining the cooperation of others can be difficult. Give a specific example of when you had to do that, and what challenges you faced. What was the outcome? What was the long-term impact on your ability to work with this person?

- Please give me your best example of working cooperatively as a team member to accomplish an important goal. What was the goal or objective? What was your role in achieving this objective? To what extent did you interact with others on this project?

- Tell me about a time when your coworkers gave you feedback about your actions. How did you respond? What changes did you make?

- Describe a project you were responsible for that required a lot of interaction with people over a long period of time.

- How have you recognized and rewarded a team player in the past? What was the situation?

- Tell me about a course, work experience, or extracurricular activity where you had to work closely with others. How did it go? How did you overcome any difficulties?

- Describe a problem you had in your life when someone else's help was very important to you.

Customer Orientation

- Give me a specific example of a time when you had to address an angry customer. What was the problem and what was the outcome? How would you assess your role in defusing the situation?

- Give me an example of when you initiated a change in process or operations in response to customer feedback.

- Tell me about a marketing promotion/initiative or information dissemination you developed. How did it meet the customer's need(s)?

Commitment to Continuous Quality/Process Improvement

- Tell me about a suggestion you made to improve the way job processes/operations worked. What was the result?

- Tell me about one of your workplace improvements that another department now uses.

- Give me an example when you initiated a change in process or operations.

- In your last job, what problems did you identify that had previously been overlooked? Were changes made? Who supported the changes as a result of your ideas?

- Describe something you have implemented at work. What were the steps you used to implement this?

Creativity/Innovation

- Describe the most significant or creative presentation/idea that you developed/implemented.

- Describe a time when you came up with a creative solution/idea/project/report to a problem in your past work.

- Tell me about a time when you created a new process or program that was considered risky. What was the situation and what did you do?

- Can you give me an example of how you have been creative in completing your responsibilities?

- Can you think of a situation where innovation was required at work? What did you do in this situation?

Flexibility/Adaptability to Change

- By providing examples, demonstrate that you can adapt to a wide variety of people, situations and/or environments.

- What do you do when priorities change quickly? Give me one example of when this happened.

- Tell me about a decision you made while under a lot of pressure.

- Tell me about a specific time when you were given new information that affected a decision that you had already made.

- Give me an example of a time when there was a decision to be made and procedures were not in place? What was the outcome?

- When was the last time you felt pressure on a job? How did the situation come about? How did you react? What made you decide to handle it that way? What effect, if any, did this have on your other responsibilities?

- What are some of the things your last employer could have done to keep you?

Continuous Learning/Development

- Describe a decision you made or a situation that you would have handle differently if you had to do it over again.

- When you have been made aware of, or have discovered for yourself, a problem in your work performance, what was your course of action? Can you give me an example?

- Tell me about a time when your supervisor/co-workers gave you feedback about your work/actions. What did you learn about yourself?

- What have you done to further your own professional development in the last 5 years?

- Tell me about a job that you had which required you to learn new things.

- Tell me about a recent job or experience that you would describe as a real learning experience. What did you learn from the job or the experience?

- Tell me about a time when you were asked to complete a difficult assignment even though the odds were against you. What did you learn from that experience?

- Discuss the highlights of your most recent educational experience. Did you accomplish any special achievements? What were your most difficult challenges?

- I noticed on your resume that you attended _____ training program. Please describe the training program. How have you applied what you learned to your current job?

Displays Vision

- Describe what steps/methods you have used to define/identify a vision for your unit/position.

- In your current or former position, what were your short and long-term goals? How long ago did you set them? Who else was involved in setting them? Which ones were achieved?

- How do you see your job relating to the overall goals of your present/previous organization?

- Tell me about a time when you anticipated the future and made changes to current responsibilities/operations to meet future needs.

Leadership/Initiative

- What are 3 effective leadership qualities you think are important. How have you demonstrated these qualities in your past/current position?

- Describe a situation in which you were able to use persuasion to successfully convince someone to approach things your way. What level was the person you had to persuade?

- What risks did you take in your present/previous job? Tell me about it.

- Tell me about your efforts to "sell" a new idea to your supervisor.

- Describe a leadership situation that you would handle differently if you had it to do over again.

- What one experience proved to you that you would be a capable manager?

- What have you done to develop the skills of your staff?

- Tell me about a time when you were able to provide a co-worker with recognition for the work they performed. What did you do?

- Tell me about a time when you reached out for additional responsibility.

- Tell me about a project/suggestion that you initiated. Explain how you communicated the project/suggestion.

- What have you done in your present/previous job that goes beyond what was required?

Making People Matter
Respect for Others

- Tell me about a time when you had to resolve a difference of opinion with a co-worker/customer/supervisor. How do you feel you showed respect?

- Tell me about a time when you needed to give feedback to an employee with emotional or sensitive problems. Was the outcome?

- Describe the way you handled a specific problem involving others with differing values, ideas and beliefs in your current/previous job.

Interpersonal Skills

- Give me a specific example of a time when you had to address an angry customer. What was the problem and what was the outcome?

- Tell me about the most difficult challenge you faced in trying to work cooperatively with someone who did not share the same ideas. What was your role in achieving the work objective? What was the long-term impact on your ability to get things done while working with this person?

- Describe a work situation that required you to really listen and display compassion to a co-worker/employee who was telling you about a personal/sensitive situation.

- Describe the way you handled a specific problem involving people in your last job.

Supports Diversity and Understands Related Issues

- Tell me about a time when you had to adapt to a wide variety of people by accepting/understanding their perspective.

- What have you done to further your knowledge/understanding about diversity? How have you demonstrated your learning?

- Can you recall a time when you gave feedback to a co-worker who was unaccepting of others?

- Can you recall a time when a person's cultural background affected your approach to a work situation?

- How have you handled situations in which you could not understand a customer's strong accent?

- Tell me about a time that you successfully adapted to a culturally different environment.

- Tell me about a situation in which you had to separate the person from the issue when working to resolve differences?

- How have you taken responsibility/accountability for an action that may have been offensive to the recipient?

- Tell me about a time that you had adapted your style in order to work effectively with those who were different from you.

- How have you reacted to conversations between co-workers that were clearly offensive to non-participants?

- Give examples of when your values and beliefs impacted your relationships with your co-workers.

- Tell me about a time that you evaluated your own beliefs or opinions around issues of difference.

- Tell me about a time when you avoided forming an opinion based upon a person's outward appearance.

- How have you made your voice heard in a predominantly male or female-dominated environment?

- What measures have you taken to make someone feel comfortable in an environment that was obviously uncomfortable with his or her presence?

Honesty/Fairness

- Tell me about a specific time when you had to handle a tough problem which challenged fairness or ethical issues.

- Tell me about a tough decision you made. What steps, thought processes, and considerations did you take to make an objective decision?

Builds Trust

- Think of a situation where you distrusted a co-worker/supervisor, resulting in tension between you. What steps did you take to improve the relationship?

- Keeping others informed of your progress/actions helps them feel comfortable. Tell me your methods for keeping your supervisor advised of the status on projects.

- If you can, tell me about a time when your trustworthiness was challenged. How did you react/respond?

- Give me examples of how your have acted with integrity (walked your talk) in your job/work relationship.

- Tell me about a time when you had to give feedback to an employee who displayed a lack of professionalism in their work relationships. What did you say? What standards did you set? What was the outcome?

- Setting high expectations implies you believe the employee can deliver. Give me an example of having done this.

- Trust requires personal accountability. Can you tell me about a time when you chose to trust someone? What was the outcome?

- Tell me about a time when you had to give the "benefit of the doubt" to a co-worker/supervisor. What was the outcome?

- Give me an example of when you 'went to the source' to address a conflict. Do you feel trust levels were improved as a result?

Recognizes Others' Achievements/Contributions

- Give me an example of how you and your staff have celebrated success in the past. What was the occasion?

- Tell me about a time when you were able to provide a co-worker/employee with recognition for the work they performed. What did you do?

- What consistent methods to you use to ensure that staff feel valued for their contributions?

Understands Others' Perspectives

- By providing examples, convince me that you can adapt to a wide variety of people.

- Gaining the cooperation of others can be difficult. Give a specific example when you had to do that.

- Tell me about the most difficult challenge you faced in trying to work cooperatively with someone who did not share the same ideas. What was the difference in ideas? What was the outcome? What was the long-term impact on your ability to get things done working with this person?

- Tell me about a time when you felt your staff was under too much pressure. What did you do about it?

Resolves Conflicts Constructively

- Give me an example of a time when you were able to successfully communicate with another person even when you felt the individual did not value your perspective.

- Tell me about a time when you and your previous supervisor disagreed but you still found a way to get your point across.

- Describe a time when you facilitated a creative solution to a problem between employees.

- Tell me about a recent success you had with an especially difficult employee/co-worker.

- Thinking of the most difficult person you have had to deal with, describe an interaction that illustrates that difficulty. Tell me about the last time you dealt with him/her? How did you handle the situation?

- Describe a time when you took personal accountability for a conflict and initiated contact with the individual(s) involved to explain your actions.

Positive Attitude

- What 3 specific things about your last job gave you the most satisfaction? Why?

- What have you done in your last job that makes you feel proud?

- Please think back to a time when setting a positive example had the most beneficial impact on people you worked with. How did you determine that a strong example was needed? What was the effect on the staff?

- Tell me about a time when you needed to address an employee's attitude. What did you say to that person? What was the outcome?

- Describe your best boss. Describe your worst boss.

Job Effectiveness
Planning/Organization

- Give me a specific example of a time when you did not meet a deadline. How did you handle it?

- Using a specific example of a project, tell me how you kept those involved informed of the progress.

132

- Are you better at working on many things at a time, or are you better at working on and getting results on a few specific things? Please give me two examples that illustrate this.

- Name one of your best accomplishments, including where the assignment came from, your plans in carrying it out, how you eventually did carry it out, and any obstacles you overcame.

- Of your current assignments, which do you consider to have required the greatest amount of effort with regard to planning/organization? How have you accomplished this assignment? Tell me how you handled it. How would you assess your effectiveness?

Problem Solving/Judgement

- Describe an instance when you had to think quickly to free yourself from a difficult situation.

- Tell me about a politically complex work situation in which you worked.

- Give me a specific example of a time when you used good judgement and logic in solving a problem.

- Give me an example of a time when there was a decision to be made and procedures were not in place? What was the outcome?

- How do you go about solving problems at work?

- Tell me about a specific time when you eliminated or avoided a potential problem before it happened.

- What types of problems do you most enjoy tackling? Give me some examples of such problems you faced. What did you enjoy about them?

- What types of problems do you least enjoy tackling? Give me some examples of such problems you faced. What was it about the problems that you least enjoyed?

- To whom did you turn for help the last time you had a major problem and why did you choose that person?

- In some aspects of work it is important to be free of error. Can you describe a situation where you have tried to prevent errors? What did you do? What was the outcome?

Makes Effective Decisions

- Tell me about a decision you made but wish you had done differently.

- Tell me about an experience in which you had a limited amount of time to make a difficult decision. What was the decision and the outcome/result of your decision?

- Give me an example of a time when there was a decision to be made and procedures were not in place? What was the outcome?

- Tell me about a time when you had to make an unpopular decision.

- Discuss an important decision you have made regarding work. What factors influenced your decision?

- In a current job task, what steps do you go through to ensure your decisions are correct/effective?

Takes Responsibility

- Give me an example of something you've done in previous jobs that demonstrate your willingness to work hard.

- What is the biggest error in judgement or failure you have made in a previous job? Why did you make it? How did you correct the problem?

- Tell me about a time when your supervisor criticized your work. How did you respond?

- Tell me about a time when you took responsibility for an error and were held personally accountable.

Achieves Results

- Describe a situation in which you were able to use persuasion to successfully convince someone to approach things your way.

- Give me an example of an important goal that you had set in the past, and tell me about your success in reaching it.

- What projects were accomplished during your previous job? How were these accomplished? What experiences did you have when meeting deadlines for project completion? Explain.

- Are you better at working on many things at a time, or are you better at working on and getting results on a few specific things? Please give me two examples that illustrate this.

- What do you consider your greatest accomplishments in your current/previous position?

Communicates Effectively

- Describe a situation in which you were able to use persuasion to successfully convince someone to see things your way.

- Tell me about a time in which you had to use your written communication skills in order to get an important point across.

- Give me an example of a time when you were able to successfully communicate with another person even when that individual may not have agreed with your perspective.

- Give me a specific example of a time when you had to handle an angry customer. What was the problem and what was the outcome?

- Tell me about a time when you and your current/previous supervisor disagreed but you still found a way to get your point across.

- Tell me about your efforts to "sell" a new idea to your supervisor.

- How do you make your feelings known when you disagree with the views of your staff?

- What have you done to improve your verbal communication skills?

- What have you done to improve your listening skills?

- Tell me how you kept your supervisor advised of the status on projects.

- How have you assessed your behavioral messages and what have you learned about yourself as a result?

Dependability/Attendance

- Give me a specific example of a time when you did not meet a deadline. How did you handle it?

- We all face times when personal issues pull us away from work responsibilities. If possible, tell me about a time when your dependability or attendance was challenged. How did you handle it and/or remain accountable or involved in work? How long did the situation last?

Job/Organizational Knowledge

- Describe how your position contributes to your organization's/unit's goals. What are the goal's/unit's mission?

- Tell me how you keep your job knowledge current with the ongoing changes in the industry.

Productivity

- Give me an example of an important goal that you had set in the past, and tell me about your success in reaching it.

- Tell me about a time when you had to complete multiple tasks/projects within a tight timeline.

- Tell me about a time when you had to go above and beyond the call of duty in order to get a job done.

- Give me a specific example of a time when you did not meet a deadline. How did you handle it?

- Give me two examples of things you've done in previous jobs that demonstrate your willingness to work hard.

- Describe a course, project, or work experience that was complex. What kind of follow-up did you undertake? How much time was spent on unexpected difficulties?

Additional Factors for Supervisors
Coaches/Counsels/Evaluates Staff

- Give me an example of a time when you helped a staff member accept change and make the necessary adjustments to move forward. What were the change/transition skills that you used?

- Tell me about a specific time when you had to handle a tough morale problem.

- Tell me about a time when you had to take disciplinary action with someone you supervised.

- Tell me about a time when you had to tell a staff member that you were dissatisfied with his or her work.

- Tell me about a time when you had to handle a highly emotional employee.

- Discuss a work situation in which you felt you successfully directed the work of others.

- Tell me about a time when your department was going through long-term changes or working on a long-term project. What did you do to keep your staff focused?

Identifies Areas for and Supports Employee Development Opportunities

- What have you done to develop the skills of your staff? How many of your employees have received training (any form) during the past year? What were the specific topic areas? Did they ask for the training or did your suggest it to them?

- Tell me about a specific development plan that you created and carried out with one or more of your employees. What was the specific situation? What were the components of the development plan? How long was the time frame from start to finish? What was the outcome?

Encourages Teamwork and Group Achievement

- Please tell me about your most successful attempt to encourage others to take action and get the job done. What led you to take these actions? Exactly how did you encourage others to take action or responsibility? What was the result of your efforts? Did anyone comment on your actions? Who? What was said? How often have you taken this type of action in the past six months?

- Tell me about a time when you needed to have co-workers working on a project who normally have different work styles/ideas. How did you pull them together?

Leads Change/Achieves Support of Objectives

- Tell me about a time when you were responsible for hiring and orientating a new employee. What did you do to help them adjust?

- Tell me about a time when your department was going through long-term changes or working on a long-term project. What did you do to keep your staff focused?

- Give me an example of a time when you helped a staff member accept change and make the necessary adjustments to move forward.

Enables and Empowers Staff

- Tell me about a time when you needed to delegate parts of a large assignment. How did you decide whom to distribute them to? What problems occurred? What was the outcome?

- What specific information do/did you share with your staff, how often do you share this information and why?

- Give me a specific example of how you have empowered your staff to make independent decisions.

- Tell me about the expectations you create for staff. What are they? What factors do you consider in setting/communicating expectations?

Strives to Achieve Diverse Staff at all Levels

- Give me a specific example of how you have helped create an environment where differences are valued, encouraged and supported.

- What have you done to support diversity in your unit?

Understands Diversity Issues and Creates Supportive Environment for Diverse Employees

- Tell me about the specific talents and contributions of your team/staff and how you have utilized these qualities to increase the effectiveness of the unit.

- What have you done to support diversity in your unit?

- Can you recall a time when you gave feedback to an employee who was unaccepting of others?

Appendix A: Government Job Listings

Federal Government (Highest Paying):

http://www.usajobs.opm.gov

State and Local Jobs (where websites are available):

http://statejobs.com/gov.html (if the links below do not work)

Alabama	Montana
Alaska	Nebraska
Arizona	New Hampshire
Arkansas	New Jersey
California	New Mexico
Colorado	New York
Connecticut	Nevada
Delaware	North Carolina
Florida	North Dakota
Georgia	Ohio
Hawaii	Oklahoma
Idaho	Oregon
Illinois	Pennsylvania
Indiana	Rhode Island
Iowa	South Carolina
Kansas	South Dakota
Kentucky	Tennessee
Louisiana	Texas
Maine	Utah
Maryland	Vermont
Massachusetts	Virginia
Michigan	Washington
Minnesota	West Virginia
Mississippi	Wisconsin
Missouri	Wyoming

Appendix B: Cover Letter Template

Your Address

Your Address

Date

Contact Name

Contact Title

Company Name

Company Address 1

Company Address 2

Company Address 3

Dear Mr./Ms. Contact Last Name:

First Paragraph: Indicate your interest in the organization, its products or services. State your source of information about the employer (Internet, news media, career center, employer directory, i.e., Peterson's Job Opportunities in Engineering and Technology, or employment service). If you were referred, indicate your contact's name, title, and employer where applicable.

Second Paragraph: Outline your strongest qualifications, focusing on the broader occupational and/or organizational dimensions. Include academic background, work experience, internships, participation in cooperative education, or any extracurricular involvement/leadership positions. Highlight strengths, skills, and accomplishments, describing how your qualifications match the work environment.

Third Paragraph: Refer the reader to the enclosed resume or employment application which summarizes your qualifications, training, experiences, and education. Be careful not to repeat your resume entirely in your letter. Provide details and explanations that are not found on your resume. Do some personal marketing here. Convince the employer you have the personal qualities and motivation to make a contribution to the organization. Do not inquire about what the organization can offer.

Concluding Paragraph: Suggest an action plan. Indicate that you will call during a specific time period to discuss interview possibilities. Indicate your flexibility. Repeat an e-mail address or a phone number (or add a different address or number where you can be reached, if appropriate). You may even want to ask if the company will be recruiting in your area, or if any additional information or references from you would be helpful. Finally, thank the reader for his/her time and consideration.

Respectfully,

Your Name

Enclosure

Appendix C: Model Resume

JOHN SMITH
123 Any Street
Any City, Any State 12345
123-456-7890
e-mail: jsmith@anywhere.com

OBJECTIVE

To obtain a position as a Distribution Manager that utilizes my 7 years of distribution and logistics management experience, my experience founding and managing a small business, and my bachelor's degree in business administration.

PROFESSIONAL SUMMARY

Experience with successfully managing all aspects of a large distribution center including implementing automated distribution systems; selecting, managing and training staff; developing and managing the departmental budget; establishing and monitoring productivity goals; and leading cross-functional teams on key projects. Have designed the layout, organization, processes, and procedures for a distribution facility. Proven leadership skills gained from managing a large distribution center as well as founding and managing a multi-million dollar business.

EXPERIENCE

General Manager, Distribution
ABC Companies, Any City, Any State, 1989 – 1999.

- Reporting to the Executive Vice President of Operations, responsible for managing all aspects of operations for a 270,000 SF distribution center with a 94-person staff and a $3.4 million budget.

- Processed 8 million units annually while managing 5,700 SKUs to supply appropriate product to over 500 different locations during off-peak times and 750 locations during peak times.

- Developed operating budget for Distribution Center based on detailed forecasts and managed Distribution Center to operate effectively within the operating budget.

- Reduced Distribution Center expenses by more than $1.5 million, a 30% reduction, over a 2-year period while maintaining productivity levels, service quality, and inventory accuracy.

- Designed an employee productivity improvement incentive program that resulted in a 28% increase in productivity.

- Developed a seasonal staffing program that eliminated the need for temporary labor resulting in a $500,000 savings.

- Directed the successful start-up of a new distribution facility achieving within the first quarter of operation a distribution volume that exceeded plan by over 200%.

- Selected and implemented a warehouse management software system, trained users, and developed procedures to integrate the computerized system.

- Led cross-functional team integrating the distribution system with a new database merchandising system.

- *141* -

- Redesigned receiving and picking operations to incorporate an automated system completing the project on time and under budget.

Founder and President
XYZ, Inc., Any City, Any State, 1982 – 1989.

- Founded and led a 14-employee company generating a peak of $4.7 million in annual sales.

- Responsible for residential construction projects for over 150 new single-family homes.

- Managed the complete project including bidding, design, scheduling, purchasing, subcontracting, and customer service.

- Scheduled subcontractor activities and oversaw multiple subcontractors to ensure construction projects were completed on time and within budget.

- Developed, marketed and sold residential real estate by establishing affiliations with CDE Group, A-1Bank, Top Realty, and Best Realty.

EDUCATION

Any University, Any City, Any State
Bachelor of Arts, Business Administration

SKILLS

DMS, MS Office, Spreadsheet Software, ORACLE

PROFESSIONAL DEVELOPMENT

World Class Logistics, CLM Annual Conference
Supply Chain Management, CLM Annual Conference

PROFESSIONAL AFFILIATIONS

Member, Council of Logistics Management

Special Report: How to Overcome Your Fear of Math

If this article started by saying "Math," many of us would feel a shiver crawl up our spines, just by reading that simple word. Images of torturous years in those crippling desks of the math classes can become so vivid to our consciousness that we can almost smell those musty textbooks, and see the smudges of the #2 pencils on our fingers.

If you are still a student, feeling the impact of these sometimes overwhelming classroom sensations, you are not alone if you get anxious at just the thought of taking that compulsory math course. Does your heart beat just that much faster when you have to split the bill for lunch among your friends with a group of your friends? Do you truly believe that you simply don't have the brain for math? Certainly you're good at other things, but math just simply isn't one of them? Have you ever avoided activities, or other school courses because they appear to involve mathematics, with which you're simply not comfortable?

If any one or more of these "symptoms" can be applied to you, you could very well be suffering from a very real condition called "Math Anxiety."

It's not at all uncommon for people to think that they have some sort of math disability or allergy, when in actuality, their block is a direct result of the way in which they were taught math!

In the late 1950's with the dawning of the space age, New Math - a new "fuzzy math" reform that focuses on higher-order thinking, conceptual understanding and solving problems - took the country by storm. It's now becoming ever more clear that teachers were not supplied with the correct, practical and effective way in which they should be teaching new math so that students will understand the methods comfortably. So is it any wonder that so many students struggled so deeply, when their teachers were required to change their entire math systems without the foundation of proper training? Even if you have not been personally, directly affected by that precise event, its impact is still as rampant as ever.

Basically, the math teachers of today are either the teachers who began teaching the new math in the first place (without proper training) or they are the students of the math teachers who taught new math without proper training. Therefore, unless they had a unique, exceptional teacher, their primary, consistent examples of teaching math have been teachers using methods that are not conducive to the general understanding of the entire class. This explains why your discomfort (or fear) of math is not at all rare.

It is very clear why being called up to the chalk board to solve a math problem is such a common example of a terrifying situation for students - and it has very little to do with a fear of being in front of the class. Most of us have had a minimum of one humiliating experience while standing with chalk dusted fingers, with the eyes of every math student piercing through us. These are the images that haunt us all the way through adulthood. But it does not mean that we cannot learn math. It just means that we could be developing a solid case of math anxiety.

But what exactly is math anxiety? It's an very strong emotional sensation of anxiety, panic, or fear that people feel when they think about or must apply their ability to understand mathematics. Sufferers of math anxiety frequently believe that they are incapable of doing activities or taking classes that involve math skills. In fact, some people with math anxiety have developed such a fear that it has become a phobia; aptly named math phobia.

The incidence of math anxiety, especially among college students, but also among high school students, has risen considerably over the last 10 years, and currently this increase shows no signs of slowing down. Frequently students will even chose their college majors and programs based specifically on how little math will be compulsory for the completion of the degree.

The prevalence of math anxiety has become so dramatic on college campuses that many of these schools have special counseling programs that are designed to assist math anxious students to deal with their discomfort and their math problems.

Math anxiety itself is not an intellectual problem, as many people have been lead to believe; it is, in fact, an emotional problem that stems from improper math teaching techniques that have slowly built and reinforced these feelings. However, math anxiety can result in an intellectual problem when its symptoms interfere with a person's ability to learn and understand math.

The fear of math can cause a sort of "glitch" in the brain that can cause an otherwise clever person to stumble over even the simplest of math problems. A study by Dr. Mark H. Ashcraft of Cleveland State University in Ohio showed that college students who usually perform well, but who suffer from math anxiety, will suffer from fleeting lapses in their working memory when they are asked to perform even the most basic mental arithmetic. These same issues regarding memory were not present in the same students when they were required to answer questions that did not involve numbers. This very clearly demonstrated that the memory phenomenon is quite specific to only math.

So what exactly is it that causes this inhibiting math anxiety? Unfortunately it is not as simple as one answer, since math anxiety doesn't have one specific cause. Frequently math anxiety can result of a student's either negative experience or embarrassment with math or a math teacher in previous years.

These circumstances can prompt the student to believe that he or she is somehow deficient in his or her math abilities. This belief will consistently lead to a poor performance in math tests and courses in general, leading only to confirm the beliefs of the student's inability. This particular phenomenon is referred to as the "self-fulfilling prophecy" by the psychological community. Math anxiety will result in poor performance, rather than it being the other way around.

Dr. Ashcraft stated that math anxiety is a "It's a learned, almost phobic, reaction to math," and that it is not only people prone to anxiety, fear, or panic who can develop math anxiety. The image alone of doing math problems can send the blood pressure and heart rate to race, even in the calmest person.

The study by Dr. Ashcraft and his colleague Elizabeth P. Kirk, discovered that students who suffered from math anxiety were frequently stumped by issues of even the most basic math rules, such as "carrying over" a number, when performing a sum, or "borrowing" from a number when doing a subtraction. Lapses such as this occurred only on working memory questions involving numbers.

To explain the problem with memory, Ashcraft states that when math anxiety begins to take its effect, the sufferer experiences a rush of thoughts, leaving little room for the focus required to perform even the simplest of math problems. He stated that "you're draining away the energy you need for solving the problem by worrying about it."

The outcome is a "vicious cycle," for students who are sufferers of math anxiety. As math anxiety is developed, the fear it promotes stands in the way of learning, leading to a decrease in self-confidence in the ability to perform even simple arithmetic.

A large portion of the problem lies in the ways in which math is taught to students today. In the US, students are frequently taught the rules of math, but rarely will they learn why a specific approach to a math problems work. Should students be provided with a foundation of "deeper understanding" of math, it may prevent the development of phobias.

Another study that was published in the Journal of Experimental Psychology by Dr. Jamie Campbell and Dr. Qilin Xue of the University of Saskatchewan in Saskatoon, Canada, reflected the same concepts. The researchers in this study looked at university students who were educated in Canada and China, discovering that the Chinese students could generally outperform the Canadian-educated students when it came to solving complex math problems involving procedural knowledge - the ability to know how to solve a math problem, instead of simply having ideas memorized.

A portion of this result seemed to be due to the use of calculators within both elementary and secondary schools; while Canadians frequently used them, the Chinese students did not.

However, calculators were not the only issue. Since Chinese-educated students also outperformed Canadian-educated students in complex math, it is suggested that cultural factors may also have an impact. However, the short-cut of using the calculator may hinder the development of the problem solving skills that are key to performing well in math.

Though it is critical that students develop such fine math skills, it is easier said than done. It would involve an overhaul of the training among all elementary and secondary educators, changing the education major in every college.

Math Myths

One problem that contributes to the progression of math anxiety, is the belief of many math myths. These erroneous math beliefs include the following:

Men are better in math than women - however, research has failed to demonstrate that there is any difference in math ability between the sexes.

There is a single best way to solve a math problem - however, the majority of math problems can be solved in a number of different ways. By saying that there is only one way to solve a math problem, the thinking and creative skills of the student are held back.

Some people have a math mind, and others do not - in truth, the majority of people have much more potential for their math capabilities than they believe of themselves.

It is a bad thing to count by using your fingers - counting by using fingers has actually shown that an understanding of arithmetic has been established.

People who are skilled in math can do problems quickly in their heads - in actuality, even math professors will review their example problems before they teach them in their classes.

The anxieties formed by these myths can frequently be perpetuated by a range of mind games that students seem to play with themselves. These math mind games include the following beliefs:

I don't perform math fast enough - actually everyone has a different rate at which he or she can learn. The speed of the solving of math problems is not important as long as the student can solve it.

I don't have the mind for math - this belief can inhibit a student's belief in him or herself, and will therefore interfere with the student's real ability to learn math.

I got the correct answer, but it was done the wrong way - there is no single best way to complete a math problem. By believing this, a student's creativity and overall understanding of math is hindered.

If I can get the correct answer, then it is too simple - students who suffer from math anxiety frequently belittle their own abilities when it comes to their math capabilities.

Math is unrelated to my "real" life - by freeing themselves of the fear of math, math anxiety sufferers are only limiting their choices and freedoms for the rest of their life.

Fortunately, there are many ways to help those who suffer from math anxiety. Since math anxiety is a learned, psychological response to doing or thinking about math, that interferes with the sufferer's ability to understand and perform math, it is not at all a reflection of the sufferer's true math sills and abilities.

Helpful Strategies

Many strategies and therapies have been developed to help students to overcome their math anxious responses. Some of these helpful strategies include the following:

Reviewing and learning basic arithmetic principles, techniques and methods. Frequently math anxiety is a result of the experience of many students with early negative situations, and these students have never truly developed a strong base in basic arithmetic, especially in the case of multiplication and fractions. Since math is a discipline that is built on an accumulative foundation, where the concepts are built upon gradually from simpler concepts, a student who has not achieved a solid basis in arithmetic will experience difficulty in learning higher order math. Taking a remedial math course, or a short math course that focuses on arithmetic can often make a considerable difference in reducing the anxious response that math anxiety sufferers have with math.

Becoming aware of any thoughts, actions and feelings that are related to math and responses to math. Math anxiety has a different effect on different students. Therefore it is very important to become familiar with any reactions that the math anxiety sufferer may have about him/herself and the situation when math has been encountered. If the sufferer becomes aware of any irrational or unrealistic thoughts, it's possible to better concentrate on replacing these thoughts with more positive and realistic ones.

Find help! Math anxiety, as we've mentioned, is a learned response, that is reinforced repeatedly over a period of time, and is therefore not something that can be eliminated instantaneously. Students can more effectively reduce their anxious responses with the help of many different services that are readily available. Seeking the assistance of a psychologist or counselor, especially one with a specialty in math anxiety, can assist the sufferer in performing an analysis of his/her psychological response to math, as well as learning anxiety management skills, and developing effective coping strategies. Other great tools are tutors, classes that teach better abilities to take better notes in math class, and other math learning aids.

Learning the mathematic vocabulary will instantly provide a better chance for understanding new concepts. One major issue among students is the lack of understanding of the terms and vocabulary that are common jargon within math classes. Typically math classes will utilize words in a completely different way from the way in which they are utilized in all other subjects. Students easily mistake their lack of understanding the math terms with their mathematical abilities.

Learning anxiety reducing techniques and methods for anxiety management. Anxiety greatly interferes with a student's ability to concentrate, think clearly, pay attention, and remember new concepts. When these same students can learn to relax, using anxiety management techniques, the student can regain his or her ability to control his or her emotional and physical symptoms of anxiety that interfere with the capabilities of mental processing.

Working on creating a positive overall attitude about mathematics. Looking at math with a positive attitude will reduce anxiety through the building of a positive attitude.

Learning to self-talk in a positive way. Pep talking oneself through a positive self talk can greatly assist in overcoming beliefs in math myths or the mind games that may be played. Positive self-talking is an effective way to replace the negative thoughts - the ones that create the anxiety. Even if the sufferer doesn't believe the statements at first, it plants a positive seed in the subconscious, and allows a positive outlook to grow.

Beyond this, students should learn effective math class, note taking and studying techniques. Typically, the math anxious students will avoid asking questions to save themselves from embarrassment. They will sit in the back of classrooms, and refrain from seeking assistance from the professor. Moreover, they will put off studying for math until the very last moment, since it causes them such substantial discomfort. Alone, or a combination of these negative behaviors work only to reduce the anxiety of the students, but in reality, they are actually building a substantially more intense anxiety.

There are many different positive behaviors that can be adopted by math anxious students, so that they can learn to better perform within their math classes.

Sit near the front of the class. This way, there will be fewer distractions, and there will be more of a sensation of being a part of the topic of discussion.

If any questions arise, ASK! If one student has a question, then there are certain to be others who have the same question but are too nervous to ask - perhaps because they have not yet learned how to deal with their own math anxiety.

Seek extra help from the professor after class or during office hours.

Prepare, prepare, prepare - read textbook material before the class, do the homework and work out any problems available within the textbook. Math skills are developed through practice and repetition, so the more practice and repetition, the better the math skills.

Review the material once again after class, to repeat it another time, and to reinforce the new concepts that were learned.

Beyond these tactics that can be taken by the students themselves, teachers and parents need to know that they can also have a large impact on the reduction of math anxiety within students.

As parents and teachers, there is a natural desire to help students to learn and understand how they will one day utilize different math techniques within their everyday lives. But when the student or teacher displays the symptoms of a person who has had nightmarish memories regarding math, where hesitations then develop in the instruction of students, these fears are automatically picked up by the students and commonly adopted as their own. However, it is possible for teachers and parents to move beyond their own fears to better educate students by overcoming their own hesitations and learning to enjoy math.

Begin by adopting the outlook that math is a beautiful, imaginative or living thing. Of course, we normally think of mathematics as numbers that can be added or subtracted, multiplied or divided, but that is simply the beginning of it.

By thinking of math as something fun and imaginative, parents and teachers can teach children different ways to manipulate numbers, for example in balancing a checkbook. Parents rarely tell their children that math is everywhere around us; in nature, art, and even architecture. Usually, this is because they were never shown these relatively simple connections. But that pattern can break very simply through the participation of parents and teachers.

The beauty and hidden wonders of mathematics can easily be emphasized through a focus that can open the eyes of students to the incredible mathematical patterns that arise everywhere within the natural world. Observations and discussions can be made into things as fascinating as spider webs, leaf patterns, sunflowers and even coastlines. This makes math not only beautiful, but also inspiring and (dare we say) fun!

Pappas Method

For parents and teachers to assist their students in discovering the true wonders of mathematics, the techniques of Theoni Pappas can easily be applied, as per her popular and celebrated book "Fractals, Googols and Other Mathematical Tales." Pappas used to be a math phobia sufferer and created a fascinating step-by-step program for parents and teachers to use in order to teach students the joy of math.

Her simple, constructive step-by-step program goes as follows:
Don't let your fear of math come across to your kids - Parents must be careful not to perpetuate the mathematical myth - that math is only for specially talented "math types." Strive not to make comments like; "they don't like math" or "I have never been good at math." When children overhear comments like these from their primary role models they begin to dread math before even considering a chance of experiencing its wonders. It is important to encourage your children to read and explore the rich world of mathematics, and to practice mathematics without imparting negative biases.

Don't immediately associate math with computation (counting) - It is very important to realize that math is not just numbers and computations, but a realm of exciting ideas that touch every part of our lives -from making a telephone call to how the hair grows on someone's head. Take your children outside and point out real objects that display math concepts. For example, show them the symmetry of a leaf or angles on a building. Take a close look at the spirals in a spider web or intricate patterns of a snowflake.

Help your child understand why math is important - Math improves problem solving, increases competency and should be applied in different ways. It's the same as reading. You can learn the basics of reading without ever enjoying a novel. But, where's the excitement in that? With math, you could stop with the basics. But why when there is so much more to be gained by a fuller Understanding? Life is so much more enriching when we go beyond the basics. Stretch your children's minds to become involved in mathematics in ways that will not only be practical but also enhance their lives.

Make math as "hands on" as possible - Mathematicians participate in mathematics. To really experience math encourage your child to dig in and tackle problems in creative ways. Help them learn how to manipulate numbers using concrete references they understand as well as things they can see or touch. Look for patterns everywhere, explore shapes and symmetries. How many octagons do you see each day on the way to the grocery store? Play math puzzles and games and then encourage your child to try to invent their own. And, whenever possible, help your child realize a mathematical conclusion with real and tangible results. For example, measure out a full glass of juice with a measuring cup and then ask your child to drink half. Measure what is left. Does it measure half of a cup?

Read books that make math exciting:

Fractals, Googols and Other Mathematical Tales introduces an animated cat who explains fractals, tangrams and other mathematical concepts you've probably never heard of to children in terms they can understand. This book can double as a great text book by using one story per lesson.

A Wrinkle in Time is a well-loved classic, combining fantasy and science.

The Joy of Mathematics helps adults explore the beauty of mathematics that is all around.

The Math Curse is an amusing book for 4-8 year olds.

The Gnarly Gnews is a free, humorous bi-monthly newsletter on mathematics.

The Phantom Tollbooth is an Alice in Wonderland-style adventure into the worlds of words and numbers.

Use the internet to help your child explore the fascinating world of mathematics.

Web Math provides a powerful set of math-solvers that gives you instant answers to the stickiest problems.

Math League has challenging math materials and contests for fourth grade and above.

Silver Burdett Ginn Mathematics offers Internet-based math activities for grades K-6.

The Gallery of Interactive Geometry is full of fascinating, interactive geometry activities.

Math is very much like a language of its own. And like any second language, it will get rusty if it is not practiced enough. For that reason, students should always be looking into new ways to keep understanding and brushing up on their math skills, to be certain that foundations do not crumble, inhibiting the learning of new levels of math.

There are many different books, services and websites that have been developed to take the fear out of math, and to help even the most uncertain student develop self confidence in his or her math capabilities.

There is no reason for math or math classes to be a frightening experience, nor should it drive a student crazy, making them believe that they simply don't have the "math brain" that is needed to solve certain problems.

There are friendly ways to tackle such problems and it's all a matter of dispelling myths and creating a solid math foundation.

Concentrate on re-learning the basics and feeling better about yourself in math, and you'll find that the math brain you've always wanted, was there all along.

Secret Key #1 - Time is Your Greatest Enemy

Pace Yourself

Wear a watch. At the beginning of the test, check the time (or start a chronometer on your watch to count the minutes), and check the time after every few questions to make sure you are "on schedule."

If you are forced to speed up, do it efficiently. Usually one or more answer choices can be eliminated without too much difficulty. Above all, don't panic. Don't speed up and just begin guessing at random choices. By pacing yourself, and continually monitoring your progress against your watch, you will always know exactly how far ahead or behind you are with your available time. If you find that you are one minute behind on the test, don't skip one question without spending any time on it, just to catch back up. Take 15 fewer seconds on the next four questions, and after four questions you'll have caught back up. Once you catch back up, you can continue working each problem at your normal pace.

Furthermore, don't dwell on the problems that you were rushed on. If a problem was taking up too much time and you made a hurried guess, it must be difficult. The difficult questions are the ones you are most likely to miss anyway, so it isn't a big loss. It is better to end with more time than you need than to run out of time.

Lastly, sometimes it is beneficial to slow down if you are constantly getting ahead of time. You are always more likely to catch a careless mistake by working more slowly than quickly, and among very high-scoring test takers (those who are likely to have lots of time left over), careless errors affect the score more than mastery of material.

Secret Key #2 - Guessing is not Guesswork

You probably know that guessing is a good idea - unlike other standardized tests, there is no penalty for getting a wrong answer. Even if you have no idea about a question, you still have a 20-25% chance of getting it right.

Most test takers do not understand the impact that proper guessing can have on their score. Unless you score extremely high, guessing will significantly contribute to your final score.

Monkeys Take the Test

What most test takers don't realize is that to insure that 20-25% chance, you have to guess randomly. If you put 20 monkeys in a room to take this test, assuming they answered once per question and behaved themselves, on average they would get 20-25% of the questions correct. Put 20 test takers in the room, and the average will be much lower among guessed questions. Why?

1. The test writers intentionally writes deceptive answer choices that "look" right. A test taker has no idea about a question, so picks the "best looking" answer, which is often wrong. The monkey has no idea what looks good and what doesn't, so will consistently be lucky about 20-25% of the time.

2. Test takers will eliminate answer choices from the guessing pool based on a hunch or intuition. Simple but correct answers often get excluded, leaving a 0% chance of being correct. The monkey has no clue, and often gets lucky with the best choice.

This is why the process of elimination endorsed by most test courses is flawed and detrimental to your performance- test takers don't guess, they make an ignorant stab in the dark that is usually worse than random.

$5 Challenge

Let me introduce one of the most valuable ideas of this course- the $5 challenge:

You only mark your "best guess" if you are willing to bet $5 on it.

You only eliminate choices from guessing if you are willing to bet $5 on it.

Why $5? Five dollars is an amount of money that is small yet not insignificant, and can really add up fast (20 questions could cost you $100). Likewise, each answer choice on one question of the test will have a small impact on your overall score, but it can really add up to a lot of points in the end.

The process of elimination IS valuable. The following shows your chance of guessing it right:

If you eliminate wrong answer choices until only this many answer choices remain:	1	2	3
Chance of getting it correct:	100%	50%	33%

However, if you accidentally eliminate the right answer or go on a hunch for an incorrect answer, your chances drop dramatically: to 0%. By guessing among all the answer choices, you are GUARANTEED to have a shot at the right answer.

That's why the $5 test is so valuable- if you give up the advantage and safety of a pure guess, it had better be worth the risk.

What we still haven't covered is how to be sure that whatever guess you make is truly random. Here's the easiest way:

Always pick the first answer choice among those remaining.

Such a technique means that you have decided, **before you see a single test question**, exactly how you are going to guess- and since the order of choices tells you nothing about which one is correct, this guessing technique is perfectly random.

This section is not meant to scare you away from making educated guesses or eliminating choices- you just need to define when a choice is worth eliminating. The $5 test, along with a pre-defined random guessing strategy, is the best way to make sure you reap all of the benefits of guessing.

Secret Key #3 - Practice Smarter, Not Harder

Many test takers delay the test preparation process because they dread the awful amounts of practice time they think necessary to succeed on the test. We have refined an effective method that will take you only a fraction of the time.

There are a number of "obstacles" in your way to succeed. Among these are answering questions, finishing in time, and mastering test-taking strategies. All must be executed on the day of the test at peak performance, or your score will suffer. The test is a mental marathon that has a large impact on your future.

Just like a marathon runner, it is important to work your way up to the full challenge. So first you just worry about questions, and then time, and finally strategy:

Success Strategy

1. Find a good source for practice tests.
2. If you are willing to make a larger time investment, consider using more than one study guide- often the different approaches of multiple authors will help you "get" difficult concepts.
3. Take a practice test with no time constraints, with all study helps "open book." Take your time with questions and focus on applying strategies.
4. Take a practice test with time constraints, with all guides "open book."
5. Take a final practice test with no open material and time limits

If you have time to take more practice tests, just repeat step 5. By gradually exposing yourself to the full rigors of the test environment, you will condition your mind to the stress of test day and maximize your success.

Secret Key #4 - Prepare, Don't Procrastinate

Let me state an obvious fact: if you take the test three times, you will get three different scores. This is due to the way you feel on test day, the level of preparedness you have, and, despite the test writers' claims to the contrary, some tests WILL be easier for you than others.

Since your future depends so much on your score, you should maximize your chances of success. In order to maximize the likelihood of success, you've got to prepare in advance. This means taking practice tests and spending time learning the information and test taking strategies you will need to succeed.

Never take the test as a "practice" test, expecting that you can just take it again if you need to. Feel free to take sample tests on your own, but when you go to take the official test, be prepared, be focused, and do your best the first time!

Secret Key #5 - Test Yourself

Everyone knows that time is money. There is no need to spend too much of your time or too little of your time preparing for the test. You should only spend as much of your precious time preparing as is necessary for you to get the score you need.

Once you have taken a practice test under real conditions of time constraints, then you will know if you are ready for the test or not.

If you have scored extremely high the first time that you take the practice test, then there is not much point in spending countless hours studying. You are already there.

Benchmark your abilities by retaking practice tests and seeing how much you have improved. Once you score high enough to guarantee success, then you are ready.

If you have scored well below where you need, then knuckle down and begin studying in earnest. Check your improvement regularly through the use of practice tests under real conditions. Above all, don't worry, panic, or give up. The key is perseverance!

Then, when you go to take the test, remain confident and remember how well you did on the practice tests. If you can score high enough on a practice test, then you can do the same on the real thing.

General Strategies

The most important thing you can do is to ignore your fears and jump into the test immediately-do not be overwhelmed by any strange-sounding terms. You have to jump into the test like jumping into a pool- all at once is the easiest way.

Make Predictions

As you read and understand the question, try to guess what the answer will be. Remember that several of the answer choices are wrong, and once you begin reading them, your mind will immediately become cluttered with answer choices designed to throw you off. Your mind is typically the most focused immediately after you have read the question and digested its contents. If you can, try to predict what the correct answer will be. You may be surprised at what you can predict.

Quickly scan the choices and see if your prediction is in the listed answer choices. If it is, then you can be quite confident that you have the right answer. It still won't hurt to check the other answer choices, but most of the time, you've got it!

Answer the Question

It may seem obvious to only pick answer choices that answer the question, but the test writers can create some excellent answer choices that are wrong. Don't pick an answer just because it sounds right, or you believe it to be true. It MUST answer the question. Once you've made your selection, always go back and check it against the question and make sure that you didn't misread the question, and the answer choice does answer the question posed.

Benchmark

After you read the first answer choice, decide if you think it sounds correct or not. If it doesn't, move on to the next answer choice. If it does, mentally mark that answer choice. This doesn't mean that you've definitely selected it as your answer choice, it just means that it's the best you've seen thus far. Go ahead and read the next choice. If the next choice is worse than the one you've already selected, keep going to the next answer choice. If the next choice is better than the choice you've already selected, mentally mark the new answer choice as your best guess.

The first answer choice that you select becomes your standard. Every other answer choice must be benchmarked against that standard. That choice is correct until proven otherwise by another answer choice beating it out. Once you've decided that no other answer choice seems as good, do one final check to ensure that your answer choice answers the question posed.

Valid Information

Don't discount any of the information provided in the question. Every piece of information may be necessary to determine the correct answer. None of the information in the question is there to throw you off (while the answer choices will certainly have information to throw you off). If two seemingly unrelated topics are discussed, don't ignore either. You can be confident there is a relationship, or it wouldn't be included in the question, and you are probably going to have to determine what is that relationship to find the answer.

Avoid "Fact Traps"

Don't get distracted by a choice that is factually true. Your search is for the answer that answers the question. Stay focused and don't fall for an answer that is true but incorrect. Always go back to the question and make sure you're choosing an answer that actually answers the question and is not just a true statement. An answer can be factually correct, but it MUST answer the question asked. Additionally, two answers can both be seemingly correct, so be sure to read all of the answer choices, and make sure that you get the one that BEST answers the question.

Milk the Question

Some of the questions may throw you completely off. They might deal with a subject you have not been exposed to, or one that you haven't reviewed in years. While your lack of knowledge about the subject will be a hindrance, the question itself can give you many clues that will help you find the correct answer. Read the question carefully and look for clues. Watch particularly for adjectives and nouns describing difficult terms or words that you don't recognize. Regardless of if you completely understand a word or not, replacing it with a synonym either provided or one you more familiar with may help you to understand what the questions are asking. Rather than wracking your mind about specific detailed information concerning a difficult term or word, try to use mental substitutes that are easier to understand.

The Trap of Familiarity

Don't just choose a word because you recognize it. On difficult questions, you may not recognize a number of words in the answer choices. The test writers don't put "make-believe" words on the test; so don't think that just because you only recognize all the words in one answer choice means that answer choice must be correct. If you only recognize words in one answer choice, then focus on that one. Is it correct? Try your best to determine if it is correct. If it is, that is great, but if it doesn't, eliminate it. Each word and answer choice you eliminate increases your chances of getting the question correct, even if you then have to guess among the unfamiliar choices.

Eliminate Answers

Eliminate choices as soon as you realize they are wrong. But be careful! Make sure you consider all of the possible answer choices. Just because one appears right, doesn't mean that the next one won't be even better! The test writers will usually put more than one good answer choice for every question, so read all of them. Don't worry if you are stuck between two that seem right. By getting down to just two remaining possible choices, your odds are now 50/50. Rather than wasting too much time, play the odds. You are guessing, but guessing wisely, because you've been able to knock out some of the answer choices that you know are wrong. If you are eliminating choices and realize that the last answer choice you are left with is also obviously wrong, don't panic. Start over and consider each choice again. There may easily be something that you missed the first time and will realize on the second pass.

Tough Questions

If you are stumped on a problem or it appears too hard or too difficult, don't waste time. Move on! Remember though, if you can quickly check for obviously incorrect answer choices, your chances of guessing correctly are greatly improved. Before you completely give up, at least try to knock out a couple of possible answers. Eliminate what you can and then guess at the remaining answer choices before moving on.

Brainstorm

If you get stuck on a difficult question, spend a few seconds quickly brainstorming. Run through the complete list of possible answer choices. Look at each choice and ask yourself, "Could this answer the question satisfactorily?" Go through each answer choice and consider it independently of the other. By systematically going through all possibilities, you may find something that you would otherwise overlook. Remember that when you get stuck, it's important to try to keep moving.

Read Carefully

Understand the problem. Read the question and answer choices carefully. Don't miss the question because you misread the terms. You have plenty of time to read each question thoroughly and make sure you understand what is being asked. Yet a happy medium must be attained, so don't waste too much time. You must read carefully, but efficiently.

Face Value

When in doubt, use common sense. Always accept the situation in the problem at face value. Don't read too much into it. These problems will not require you to make huge leaps of logic. The test writers aren't trying to throw you off with a cheap trick. If you have to go beyond creativity and make a leap of logic in order to have an answer choice answer the question, then you should look at the other answer choices. Don't overcomplicate the problem by creating theoretical relationships or explanations that will warp time or space. These are normal problems rooted in reality. It's just that the applicable relationship or explanation may not be readily apparent and you have to figure things out. Use your common sense to interpret anything that isn't clear.

Prefixes

If you're having trouble with a word in the question or answer choices, try dissecting it. Take advantage of every clue that the word might include. Prefixes and suffixes can be a huge help. Usually they allow you to determine a basic meaning. Pre- means before, post- means after, pro - is positive, de- is negative. From these prefixes and suffixes, you can get an idea of the general meaning of the word and try to put it into context. Beware though of any traps. Just because con is the opposite of pro, doesn't necessarily mean congress is the opposite of progress!

Hedge Phrases

Watch out for critical "hedge" phrases, such as likely, may, can, will often, sometimes, often, almost, mostly, usually, generally, rarely, sometimes. Question writers insert these hedge phrases to cover every possibility. Often an answer choice will be wrong simply because it leaves no room for exception. Avoid answer choices that have definitive words like "exactly," and "always".

Switchback Words

Stay alert for "switchbacks". These are the words and phrases frequently used to alert you to shifts in thought. The most common switchback word is "but". Others include although, however, nevertheless, on the other hand, even though, while, in spite of, despite, regardless of.

New Information

Correct answer choices will rarely have completely new information included. Answer choices typically are straightforward reflections of the material asked about and will directly relate to the question. If a new piece of information is included in an answer choice that doesn't even seem to relate to the topic being asked about, then that answer choice is likely incorrect. All of the information needed to answer the question is usually provided for you, and so you should not have to make guesses that are unsupported or choose answer choices that require unknown information that cannot be reasoned on its own.

Time Management

On technical questions, don't get lost on the technical terms. Don't spend too much time on any one question. If you don't know what a term means, then since you don't have a dictionary, odds are you aren't going to get much further. You should immediately recognize terms as whether or not you know them. If you don't, work with the other clues that you have, the other answer choices and terms provided, but don't waste too much time trying to figure out a difficult term.

Contextual Clues

Look for contextual clues. An answer can be right but not correct. The contextual clues will help you find the answer that is most right and is correct. Understand the context in which a phrase or statement is made. This will help you make important distinctions.

Don't Panic

Panicking will not answer any questions for you. Therefore, it isn't helpful. When you first see the question, if your mind goes blank, take a deep breath. Force yourself to mechanically go through the steps of solving the problem and using the strategies you've learned.

Pace Yourself

Don't get clock fever. It's easy to be overwhelmed when you're looking at a page full of questions, your mind is full of random thoughts and feeling confused, and the clock is ticking down faster than you would like. Calm down and maintain the pace that you have set for yourself. As long as you are on track by monitoring your pace, you are guaranteed to have enough time for yourself. When you get to the last few minutes of the test, it may seem like you won't have enough time left, but if you only have as many questions as you should have left at that point, then you're right on track!

Answer Selection

The best way to pick an answer choice is to eliminate all of those that are wrong, until only one is left and confirm that is the correct answer. Sometimes though, an answer choice may immediately look right. Be careful! Take a second to make sure that the other choices are not equally obvious. Don't make a hasty mistake. There are only two times that you should stop before checking other answers. First is when you are positive that the answer choice you have selected is correct. Second is when time is almost out and you have to make a quick guess!

Check Your Work

Since you will probably not know every term listed and the answer to every question, it is important that you get credit for the ones that you do know. Don't miss any questions through careless mistakes. If at all possible, try to take a second to look back over your answer selection and make sure you've selected the correct answer choice and haven't made a costly careless mistake (such as marking an answer choice that you didn't mean to mark). This quick double check should more than pay for itself in caught mistakes for the time it costs.

Beware of Directly Quoted Answers

Sometimes an answer choice will repeat word for word a portion of the question or reference section. However, beware of such exact duplication – it may be a trap! More than likely, the correct choice will paraphrase or summarize a point, rather than being exactly the same wording.

Slang

Scientific sounding answers are better than slang ones. An answer choice that begins "To compare the outcomes…" is much more likely to be correct than one that begins "Because some people insisted…"

Extreme Statements

Avoid wild answers that throw out highly controversial ideas that are proclaimed as established fact. An answer choice that states the "process should be used in certain situations, if…" is much more likely to be correct than one that states the "process should be discontinued completely." The first is a calm rational statement and doesn't even make a definitive, uncompromising stance, using a hedge word "if" to provide wiggle room, whereas the second choice is a radical idea and far more extreme.

Answer Choice Families

When you have two or more answer choices that are direct opposites or parallels, one of them is usually the correct answer. For instance, if one answer choice states "x increases" and another

- 168 -

answer choice states "x decreases" or "y increases," then those two or three answer choices are very similar in construction and fall into the same family of answer choices. A family of answer choices is when two or three answer choices are very similar in construction, and yet often have a directly opposite meaning. Usually the correct answer choice will be in that family of answer choices. The "odd man out" or answer choice that doesn't seem to fit the parallel construction of the other answer choices is more likely to be incorrect.